JESUS IN THE SPOTLIGHT

JOHN 1-10

KAY ARTHUR
WITH CYNDY SHEARER

HARVEST HOUSE PUBLISHERS
Eugene, Oregon 97402

Verses marked NASB are taken from the New American Standard Bible, © 1960, 1962, 1963, 1968, 1971, 1972, 1973, 1975, 1977 by The Lockman Foundation. Used by permission.

Interior design by Ty Pauls, Harvest House Publishers

Illustrations by Steve Bjorkman

Cover by Left Coast Design, Portland, Oregon

Discover 4 Yourself Bible Studies for Kids
JESUS IN THE SPOTLIGHT

Copyright © 1999 by Precept Ministries
Published by Harvest House Publishers
Eugene, Oregon 97402

ISBN 0-7369-0119-1

Printed in the United States of America.

99 00 01 02 03 / ML / 10 9 8 7 6 5 4 3 2 1

Contents

A Bible Study You Can Do!

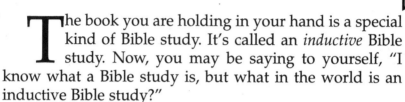

The book you are holding in your hand is a special kind of Bible study. It's called an *inductive* Bible study. Now, you may be saying to yourself, "I know what a Bible study is, but what in the world is an inductive Bible study?"

Well, the answer to that question is really pretty simple. When you study something inductively, it means that you look at it very carefully so that you can discover for yourself what it is or what it means. In other words, you don't just take someone else's word for it or go ask an expert. It means you begin by trying to figure it out for yourself. That's what we are going to do with the book of John in the Bible.

Things you'll need

▼

New American Standard Bible
Pen or Pencil
Colored Pencils
This Workbook

1

J O H N 1

Do you want to know more about Jesus? A man named John was one of His best friends. He wrote a book about Jesus' life that we call the Gospel of John. In John's book we learn a lot about Jesus—who His Father is, who His friends were, why He came, what He did, where He went, and how we can know Him better and become His friend.

Do you have a favorite book that's been made into a movie? Wouldn't it be fun to make a movie of Jesus' life? Let's imagine that we are doing just that. You can be the director, and the book of John will be our script.

As we study each chapter, we'll do what a film director would do. We'll look over each chapter to see what important things are taking place. We'll figure out who the main characters are. And we'll look closely at what John's book teaches us about Jesus and what it means to be His followers.

So, *quiet on the set,* and let's get going…

Sneak Peak

A great way to start your Bible study every day is to pray. It's important to ask God to help you understand His Word. Take a minute right now to pray that your study time would be special.

John 20:30-31 says: "Many other signs therefore Jesus also performed in the presence of the disciples, which are not written in this book; but these have been written that you may believe that Jesus is the Christ, the Son of God; and that believing you may have life in His name."

Why did John write about the signs (miracles) Jesus did?

_____

_____

What happens if you believe?

_____

_____

This is important to remember as we study.

John 20:30-31 is your memory verse for this week. Copy it out on a 3 x 5 card so you can carry it with you. Read it out loud three times each day. Your goal for the week is to memorize this Scripture!

Now, go ahead and read John, chapter 1. You'll find it on page 95.

When a director plans a movie, he first creates what is known as a storyboard. A storyboard is a rough sketch of each of the main scenes in a movie. In the spaces that follow, figure out the main events in the first chapter of John. Draw a picture or write a short description for each. We've broken the chapter into sections and done the first one as an example for you. Now it's your turn!

JOHN 1:1-18:

Jesus is the Word of God

JOHN 1:19-34:

_____

JOHN 1:35-42:

_____

JOHN 1:43-51:

_____

Good job! Now you have a good idea of what is in this chapter. Starting tomorrow we'll look more closely at some of these important ideas.

Spotlight on Key Words

On the set today, we're going to take a closer look at our script—the book of John. As we look, we're going to see some words that pop up again and again. Words that show up often are important. We call them *key words*.

KEY WORDS

✦ Key words are used over and over again

✦ Key words are important

✦ Key words are used by the writer for a reason

God   Light

Jesus   Word

John   World

Turn back to John 1 on page 95. This is where you will do your Bible study work. We call these pages Observation Worksheets. Now read verses 1-18 very carefully, looking for the key words listed below. Every time you find one of these words, mark or color it in a special way. Key words give us clues about what is most important in the passage of Scripture we are studying. Taking the time to mark them will help you figure out for yourself what the Bible is teaching.

Here are some helpful ways to mark these words. You may mark them by using different colors instead of symbols. Or you can make up your own symbols. Just remember that symbols should be simple.

Word

God

John

Light

World

These are some of the key words that appear over and over again in John's Gospel. We won't look at each key word in every chapter of our study. But once you see how much you can learn by marking key words, you might want to mark all of them throughout the book of John on your own.

For now, let's take a look at our first key word. What or who is John describing when he writes about the "Word"? (Hint: Look at verses 14-17.)

Write down five things you learn about the Word from John 1:1-18. We've done the first one for you.

1. John 1:1 *The Word was in the beginning*
2. John 1:1_____
3. John 1:1_____
4. John 1:14_____
5. John 1:14_____

Meet the Star

Today we're going to read through the whole first chapter of John again. After reading this chapter, you should be able to guess who the star of our movie is going to be. Who is it? Who is mentioned the very most?

Read the verses that follow and write out the different words that are used to describe the main character, the star, of the Gospel of John.

John 1:1   _____
John 1:9   _____
John 1:29   _____
John 1:38   _____
John 1:41   _____
John 1:49   _____
John 1:51   _____

Now, let's try to find out more about Jesus from this chapter. Every time we answer a question, we dig a little deeper into the meaning of the text.

John 1:1-2 Who was the Word with in the beginning?

_____

John 1:1 What was the Word's relationship with God?

_____

John 1:12 What right is given to a person who "receives" Jesus?

_____

John 1:12 What does it mean to "receive Him"? (Hint: Read all the way to the end of the verse.)

_____

What an Unusual Name!

In John 1:1 we read, "In the beginning was the Word, and the Word was with God, and the Word was God." What did John mean by "the Word"?

The term "the Word" can mean "message." The Bible, which is sometimes called "the Word," is God's written message about Himself to us. But in John 1:1, John wasn't talking about the Bible. He was talking about Jesus, who served as God's message about Himself to the world. When people looked at Jesus, they saw God in action. And when they heard Him speak, they heard God's words.

The Co-Star of John 1

For the last two days we have focused on the star in the first chapter of John. But there is another person who is mentioned very often in this chapter. Do you know who it is? Look at verse 6 if you can't remember. _____. This John is not the John who wrote the Gospel you're studying. It is John the Baptist.

Let's see what we can learn about this man.

John 1:6 Who sent John?

_____

John 1:7-8 What was John sent to do?

_____

John 1:15 How did John compare himself with Jesus?

_____

John 1:32-34 How did John know who Jesus was?

_____

Casting Call

In a movie there are usually lots of cast members. Some play big parts. Some play small parts. But all of the cast members are important. As you know by now, Jesus and John aren't the only two characters in the first chapter of John. In John's Gospel we'll see how Jesus talks to and helps lots of different people. Let's find out what the first people to meet Him in this Gospel said and did.

John 1:35-36 What did John the Baptist say to his disciples when he saw Jesus?

_____

John 1:37 What did John's disciples do?

_____

John 1:40-42 Two brothers met Jesus. What were their names?

_____

John 1:41 What was the first thing Andrew did after he met Jesus?

_____

John 1:43 What did Jesus say to Philip?

_____

John 1:45 What did Philip do as soon as he started following Jesus?

_____

John 1:48-49 What made Nathanael believe in Jesus?

_____

John 1:50 Nathanael thought what Jesus did was a big deal. Did Jesus think it was?

_____

It's a Wrap!

Good job! You studied the Bible for yourself this week. You learned a lot of different names for Jesus, which will give you a better idea of who He is. And you met some of the first people to follow Him. You're off to a great start!

Here's a fun idea. If you were going to be in the movie, which role would you want to play and why? Which person are you most like? Get your friends or family and cast each character in John 1. Now, act it out!

2

JOHN 2

As the director, it is now time to make plans for how you would film the second chapter of John. This time you'll need a special effects expert to help you out because John 2 tells about the first miracle Jesus did. John calls it a "sign." Do you remember why Jesus did signs? (Think about last week's memory verse.)

_____

_____

Remember, this is John's purpose or reason for writing his Gospel.

Sneak Peak

What's the first thing to do? Pray! Then read John 2 carefully. Create a storyboard of the main events of the chapter by writing a short description or drawing a picture for each section. Don't forget to write a title for that scene on the line below the box.

JOHN 2:1-11:   JOHN 2:12-25:

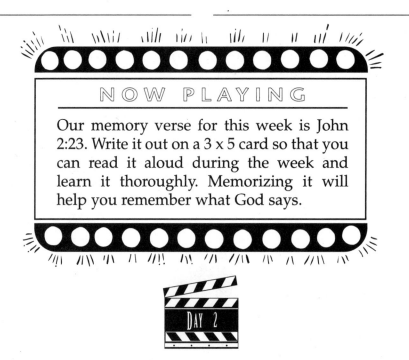

NOW PLAYING

Our memory verse for this week is John 2:23. Write it out on a 3 x 5 card so that you can read it aloud during the week and learn it thoroughly. Memorizing it will help you remember what God says.

DAY 2

Spotlight on Key Words

Read John 2 again, this time marking the key words on your Observation Worksheet (page 98). Write down one thing you learn about each key word from reading this chapter. Be sure to write down the verse or verses your answer comes from. We've done the first one for you.

Jesus   Jesus has the power to perform miracles (John 2:11).

Temple   _____

Water   _____

Wine   _____

Sign (signs)   _____

Believed   _____

Do you remember where you saw the words "Jesus," "sign," and "believed" before? They were in our memory verse for Week One that told us why John wrote his Gospel. Go back to the Observation Worksheet for John 1 (page 95). Find "Jesus" and "believe" and mark them the same way you just marked them in John 2.

So Many Questions!

One of the best ways to learn about something is by asking questions. Just like directors ask screenwriters about their movie scripts, you can ask questions about the Gospel of John.

Our starting point will be learning to ask six basic questions about the Scripture we are studying. The questions are WHO, WHAT, WHERE, WHEN, WHY, and HOW. We call these questions the "5 W's and and H." You'll be surprised at how much you can learn by asking just six questions!

Think of something fun that you did recently. If we asked you just six questions, we could learn a lot about what it was you did. Let's try it!

The fun thing I did was _____

WHO was there? _____

WHAT did you do? _____

WHERE did you do it? _____

WHEN did you do it? _____

WHY did you do it? _____

HOW did you do it? _____

See how much we learned about what you did! It's the same way when we study the Bible. Let's take a closer look at the "5 W's and an H" questions.

WHO asks questions like: Who wrote this? Who was it written to? Who do we read about in this section of Scripture? Who did this or said this?

WHAT asks questions like: What is the author talking about? What are the main things that happen in this passage?

WHEN asks questions like: When did this event happen? When did the main characters do something?

WHERE asks questions like: Where did this happen? Where did they go? Where was this said?

WHY asks questions like: Why did he say that? Why did this happen?

HOW asks questions like: How was this thing done? How did people know that something had been accomplished?

As you study John's Gospel, you'll find yourself asking these kinds of questions over and over again. But here's a hint: The answers are easy to see. You'll find them right in your Bible.

Now let's use these questions to see what we can learn from John, chapter 2.

WHO are the people mentioned in chapter 2? (Write down the names of only the main people.)

_____

_____

In John 2, Jesus goes to more than one place. List the places and the verses that record that journey.

WHERE Jesus Went   Verse

_____   _____

_____   _____

_____   _____

John 2:1 WHAT event was taking place when Jesus turned the water into wine?

_____

John 2:1 WHEN did this event take place?

_____

Keep It Simple

When you go into a movie theater, what is the first thing you notice? The movie screen, right? Big things are usually the easiest to spot. So when we study the Bible, we're going to look for the "movie screens"—the most obvious things—first. That means you don't have to look for hidden answers to questions about a passage of Scripture. The answers should be right there in the text.

John 2:2 WHY was Jesus there?

_____

John 2:9-10 HOW did the servants know the water had been changed into wine?

_____

John 2:11 WHAT does John say is special about this sign?

_____

DAY 4

Turning the Tables

After Jesus turned the water into wine at Cana, He went to Jerusalem for Passover. Read John 2:12-25 and answer these questions:

John 2:14 WHAT did Jesus see happening in the temple?

_____

John 2:15-16 WHAT did He do about it?

_____

John 2:16 WHY was Jesus so upset?

_____

John 2:20 HOW long did the Jews say it took to build the temple?

_____

John 2:19 HOW long did Jesus say it would take Him to raise up the temple?

_____

John 2:21 WHAT temple did Jesus say He would raise up?

_____

John 2:23 WHY did many people believe in Jesus' name at this time?

_____

Moneychangers

Moneychangers were bankers who sat outside the temple court in Jerusalem. They exchanged foreign money for money that the people could use to pay their temple offerings or to buy animals for sacrifices. Moneychangers charged the people a fee to do this. In Jesus' time, all Jewish men over the age of 20 had to pay a temple tax of exactly half a shekel about once a year. Because many Jews went to Jerusalem from other lands, the moneychangers would have been very busy, especially on a holiday like Passover.

Crazy Cue Cards

Throughout the Gospel of John we learn about many of the signs Jesus did. Why do you think John tells us about all these signs or miracles? Hint: Remember the verse you memorized last week! This week's memory verse also talks about the signs Jesus did.

Match Game

On the set of a movie, one person—the prompter—has the responsibility of holding up cue cards for the actors to help them know their lines. Unfortunately, that person on our set dropped her cards when a loud noise startled her.

Can you help her match the following questions to the answers on her cue cards?

QUESTIONS	ANSWERS
What did the disciples believe in?	Jerusalem
	Many
What feast were they celebrating?	
	His name
Why did they believe?	
	Because of the signs which He performed
Who believed?	
	Passover
Where was Jesus?	

It's a Wrap!

Good work! You've successfully completed another chapter of John! You've seen the first miracle (sign) Jesus did. Jesus wanted people to believe in Him, so He showed them signs to help them.

Now it's time to sit down and think about this week's work. Have you ever wondered why Jesus turned the water into wine? In Bible times, it would have been very embarrassing to run out of wine at a wedding. What does this tell you about Jesus? If Jesus cared so much about the people at the wedding, do you think He cares about your problems? All day today, why don't you talk to God, Jesus' Father, and ask Him to help you with any problems you have.

This week we also saw how Jesus cared for His Father's house, the temple. The temple is where people went to worship God, like our churches. How do you behave in church? Do you pay attention and treat your church with respect? How can you show you care for God's house?

3

JOHN 3

This week we will be looking at chapter 3 of John's Gospel. This chapter may contain the most famous verse in the entire Bible. As the director of this movie, you'll want to make sure everyone who sees your film will remember this "line," just as they do famous lines in other movies. Can you remember some favorite lines from movies you've watched? Well, John 3:16 will probably be the most important line you'll ever remember!

Sneak Peak

First let's create our storyboard by reading through chapter 3 and identifying the topic or event of each section.

JOHN 3:1-21:   **JOHN 3:22-36:**

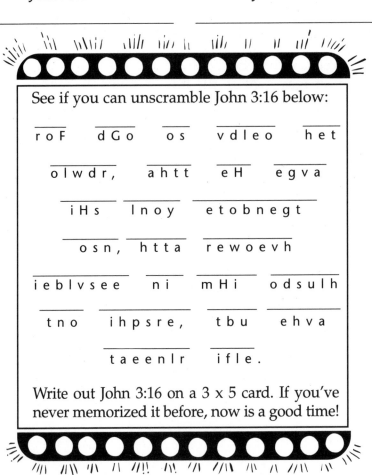

See if you can unscramble John 3:16 below:

r o F   d G o   o s   v d l e o   h e t

o l w d r,   a h t t   e H   e g v a

i H s   l n o y   e t o b n e g t

o s n,   h t t a   r e w o e v h

i e b l v s e e   n i   m H i   o d s u l h

t n o   i h p s r e,   t b u   e h v a

t a e e n l r   i f l e.

Write out John 3:16 on a 3 x 5 card. If you've never memorized it before, now is a good time!

Spotlight on Key Words

Read John 3 and color or mark with a symbol the following key words found in verses 1-21 on your Observation Worksheet (page 100):

Believes

Kingdom of God

Born or Born Again

Light

Eternal Life

Signs

Spirt

God

Jesus

Who Were the Pharisees?

As you read the Gospel of John, you will often read about the Pharisees. During the time of Jesus there were about 6000 Pharisees. These men were teachers of the law. They devoted their lives to studying the law, the first five books of the Bible.

The Pharisees took the actual laws of the Bible and turned them into a very complicated system of rules. According to these teachers, the only people who could be called "godly" were those who kept all the rules. For many of the Pharisees, obedience to their own rules became even more important than obedience to God. They did not like anyone who didn't follow all their strict rules.

Now let's answer some questions about one of the Pharisees mentioned in this chapter.

John 3:1-2 WHO came to Jesus?

_____

John 3:1 HOW is he described?

_____

John 3:2 WHY did he come to Jesus (also read John 2:23)?

_____

John 3:2 WHEN did he come to Jesus?

_____

Happy Birthday—Twice!

Beside each statement, write the name of the person who said it. Was it Jesus or Nicodemus?

"We know that You have come from God as a teacher" (John 3:2)_____

"Truly, truly I say to you" (John 3:3) _____

"How can a man be born when he is old?" (John 3:4) _____

"You must be born again" (John 3:7) _____

"Are you the teacher of Israel, and do not understand these things?" (John 3:10) _____

In John 3:5-6, Jesus contrasts two kinds of birth. Fill in the blanks.

John 3:5

    Born of w_____   Born of the S_____

John 3:6

    Born of the f_____   Born of the S_____

John 3:4 What does Nicodemus *think* Jesus is saying he must do?

_____

Two Birthdays

Isn't it great? Christians have *two* birthdays! One is the day your mother gave birth to you. That's when you were born of the flesh. Almost everybody knows their birthday. Usually you celebrate with a party or cake. And sometimes you get presents. The other birthday is the day you believe that Jesus is the Son of God and you receive Him as your Savior. (Remember John 1:12-13?) When that happens, you are "born again." That's an even bigger reason to celebrate. And the greatest present of all is that you will get to live with Jesus in heaven forever.

Nicodemus thought Jesus was talking about being born as a baby again. This is what Jesus calls being "born of the flesh." But Jesus was talking to Nicodemus about a spiritual birth, when God's Spirit comes to live inside us.

Light in the Dark

You can't shoot a movie without lights. That's why you hear the director say, "Lights! Camera! Action!" Lights come on and the cameras record the action.

The word "light" is one of your key words. Turn to your Observation Worksheet for John 3 on page 100 find the verses where you marked this word. Write out what each verse says about light.

Verse	What the Verse Says About Light
_____	_____
_____	_____
_____	_____

Let's do a little experiment called "Light in the Dark":

Materials: Bible, pencils, flashlight, batteries, hand mirror, white cardboard, black cardboard

One of the most important parts of a movie projector is the light bulb. Without it, you can't see the film. But once the projector light is turned on, the whole movie comes to life.

To begin this experiment, stand the mirror and white cardboard on their sides. Place the mirror and the white cardboard at a 90-degree angle to each other. Turn out the lights in the room. Shine a flashlight into the mirror. The light reflected on the cardboard is almost as bright as the beam of light from the flashlight.

Jesus reflects God's light like the mirror. Because Jesus is God Himself, He is the perfect reflection of God. Jesus illuminates or shows us what God is like. When we understand who Jesus is, then we "see" or know who His Father is. When Jesus said, "I am the light of the world," He was telling people that you can see God shine through Him.

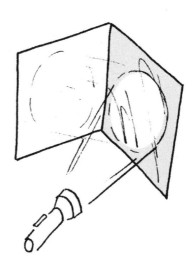

Stand the black cardboard and mirror on their sides. Place them at a 90-degree angle to each other. Turn out the lights in the room. Shine a flashlight onto the black cardboard. The blackness of the color absorbs

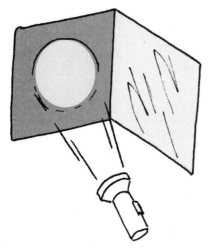

all the light. How much light reflects onto the mirror?

The blackness of the dark hides the evil that people can do. That's why evil people hate light. It exposes their acts to others so they don't want to come to Jesus. They don't want Jesus to get rid of the darkness of their sins by changing them.

Now stand the white cardboard and mirror on their sides again. Place them at a 90-degree angle to each other. Turn out the lights in the room. Shine a flashlight onto the white cardboard. How bright is the light that is reflected into the mirror?

Jesus' followers are like the white cardboard. When the light of Jesus shines on us, we can see God and reflect Him to others.

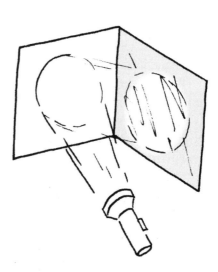

Truth or Consequences

If Nicodemus had put together a list describing the good things he'd done, what sort of things would you expect to find?

- ✓ Always went to the temple (we would say church and Sunday school)
- ✓ Kept the law
- ✓ Prayed
- ✓ Studied the Scriptures
- ✓ Gave money to the poor

You may be like Nicodemus—a very good person. You have always tried to do the right thing. You might be able to show a long list of good things you've done. But all of the good things still wouldn't get Nicodemus to heaven.

Nicodemus 2, the Sequel

Are you curious about what happened to Nicodemus after his meeting with Jesus? Check out the Scriptures below to find out.

John 7:44-52 _____

John 19:38-40 _____

Remember the reason John wrote his Gospel? (Hint: you memorized the Scripture the first week.) John 3:15-18 tells us some things about our key word "believe." Read each Scripture verse to answer each question. Then print the answer in the crossword puzzle.

Believe the Truth Crossword Puzzle

ACROSS

2. John 3:15 A person who receives eternal life does WHAT?
3. John 3:36 WHAT abides on people who do not believe in Jesus?
4. John 3:16 If you don't believe in Jesus, you will WHAT?
7. John 3:18 A person who doesn't believe in Jesus is WHAT?
8. John 3:31 WHERE did John the Baptist say Jesus came from?

DOWN

1. John 3:16 WHAT reward do those who believe in Jesus receive?
5. John 3:18 WHAT happens when you believe in Jesus?
6. John 3:33 WHAT does a person believe when he or she accepts the truth about Jesus?

(Answers are on p. 94.)

There was something separating Nicodemus from Jesus, and it was sin. God's Word says that all have sinned (Romans 3:23). To sin is to not believe Jesus is who He says He is. To sin is also to break God's commandments.

Jesus was put on a cross, and God put all our sins, all the sins of the world, on Jesus. He died for us in our place. If we don't believe this, we won't spend forever with Jesus after we die. But if we do believe this and receive Jesus, we get the gift of eternal life and will go to heaven.

It's a Wrap!

This week is over, and you've learned a lot, haven't you? You've memorized what may be the most famous line in the Bible, and you've seen how God's light can be reflected in you. And you know God loves you and wants you to be born into His family. Wow! What a great week!

Think about all you have learned by reading God's script. We are sooooo proud of you. When you finish this study, we have something we want to send you. At the back of this book, you will find a special card to fill out.

4

John 4

In the movie we're making, Jesus has already run into a lot of interesting characters. John the Baptist was a rough-and-tumble guy who ate locusts and wore camel-hair clothes (Matthew 3:4). Jesus' mother, Mary, knew her Son could do anything—even help make their friends' wedding a success. And last week you read about a very proper, very important religious man who wanted to talk to Jesus—but at night when no know one else could see him!

This week we're going to read about two other people Jesus meets as He travels around Israel. They're very different from the people He's met before. One is a woman who is part Jewish, part Gentile. The other is a royal official who has a very sick son.

Sneak Peak

First let's create our storyboard for this chapter. Read chapter 4 and write out or draw the main events in the story.

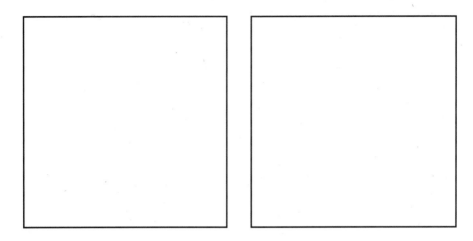

JOHN 4:1-42:   **JOHN 4:43-54:**

This week's Bible memory verse is John 4:24. Write it out on a 3 x 5 card. Read it aloud several times each day so that you can memorize it. When you say it out loud, it helps you remember it better.

Spotlight on Key Words

Now let's look at our Observation Worksheet for John 4 on page 103 and mark the key words in this chapter. Here are the words to look for:

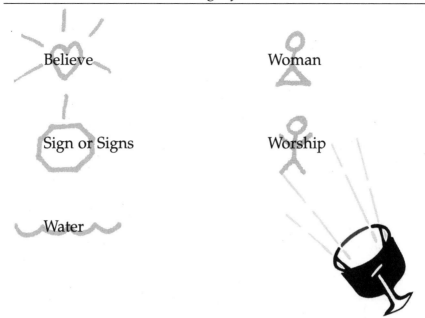

Believe

Woman

Sign or Signs

Worship

Water

Now you'll need to get ready for a scene change. As you'll see throughout the book of John, Jesus travels a lot. Today he's going to a new place, where He will meet a Samaritan woman. In order to understand their conversation, you're going to need to know something about the Samaritans.

Who Are the Samaritans?

When the Assyrians invaded Israel in 722 B.C., they took most of the educated Jewish people back to Assyria as their captives. They did leave some Jews in the land. The conquering Assyrians took over Samaria, the capital of the Northern Kingdom of Israel. Many of the Jews left in Samaria married the Assyrians. But the Assyrians were not Jewish. Anyone who is not a Jew is a called a Gentile in the Bible, and God had told the Jews *not* to marry Gentiles. The children born to these marriages were half-Gentile, half-Jewish. They were called Samaritans. They soon developed religious practices that were different from the ones commanded by the Bible.

When the rest of the Jews finally returned to their own land, they would have nothing to do with the Samaritans. In Jesus' time, Jews wouldn't walk through the Samaritans' city—they walked all the way around it. Jewish people did not even talk to Samaritans!

But Jesus, even though He was Jewish, did talk to the Samaritan woman. He took water from her and spent time talking to her and treating her with respect. Best of all, He told her who He was. Jesus wasn't going to let an old fight between Jews and Samaritans stop Him from helping someone! God cares about all people, no matter where they come from.

Now let's answer a few questions from John 4:1-42.

John 4:7 WHO are the two people who meet each other?

_____

John 4:8 WHERE are Jesus' disciples when He talks with the woman?

_____

John 4:3 WHERE was Jesus going?

_____

John 4:4 WHAT region did He have to go through to get there?

_____

John 4:5 WHAT city did Jesus stop in?

_____

No Small Parts

Sometimes characters in a movie have very small parts, but small parts add a lot to a movie. Let's take a good look at the Samaritan woman. Her part is small, but it is very important to Jesus.

John 4:7 WHAT did Jesus ask for when He met the Samaritan woman?

_____

WHY is water so important to us? List some of the things you know about water.

_____

John 4:13-14 HOW is the living water Jesus offers different from the water in the well?

_____

Living Water

In Bible times, a woman's task was to draw water for her family. All water used for cooking and cleaning was hand-carried from the main source of water in the town.

Israel is a dry country. The people and the land depend on rain and underground wells for life-giving water. No rain means no water. The people also stored the precious rainwater in cisterns. Cisterns were deep holes dug into the rocks. The cisterns often trapped more than water runoff. Animals would fall into the pits and contaminate the water. Water that collected in these pits was often dirty and stale.

The water in the cisterns was quite different from water flowing from springs. Springwater was fresh, cool, and clean. Fresh water was scarce. It was called "living water."

It takes the Samaritan woman a little while, but she slowly figures out who Jesus is. Read the following verses and write out what she knows or thinks about Him. As you do, watch how her understanding changes as they keep on talking.

John 4:9 _____

John 4:19 _____

John 4:29 _____

John 4:39-40 HOW do the people in the town respond to Jesus?

_____

DAY 4

Solve the Puzzle

Crossword Review

Read the sentence. Complete the crossword puzzle.

ACROSS

4. The woman was from _____. (John 4:7)

5. Jesus wanted a drink from the well water, but the water he could give the woman was called _____ water. (John 4:10)

6. Jesus said true worshipers shall worship the _____ . (John 4:23)

7. The woman thought Jesus was a _____. (John 4:19)

DOWN

1. The woman told Jesus that the _____was coming. (John 4:25-26)
2. When the woman returned to the village, she left her _____. (John 4:28)

3. Jesus was tired and sat beside a _____to rest. (John 4:6)

(Answers are on p. 94.)

What do you learn in John 4:20-26 about another of our key words, the word "worship"?

John 4:20   WHERE do the Samaritans worship?

_____

John 4:20   WHERE do the Jews worship?

_____

John 4:23   WHAT is true worship like? Do we have to be in a certain place at a certain time?

_____

Scene Change—Cast Change

Today we have a scene change. We're going to Galilee to meet the other interesting person you drew on your storyboard. Look at verses 43-54 to answer the questions below.

John 4:46   WHO are the main characters in this story?

_____

John 4:49   WHAT did the royal official ask Jesus to do?

_____

John 4:46   WHERE was the royal official's son?

_____

John 4:50 WHAT did Jesus do for him?

_____

John 4:54 WHAT is important about this miracle?

_____

Sometimes when a film is made about somebody's life, it will contain interviews with different people who knew that person. The interviewer can learn a lot by asking questions. In John 3–4 you read about conversations Jesus had with three people. Like a good actor, imagine that you are each of these people. Put yourself in their place. How would you think and act? How would you answer these questions?

	NICODEMUS	SAMARITAN WOMAN	ROYAL OFFICIAL
How and where did you meet Jesus?	_____	_____	_____
Where do you live?	_____	_____	_____
How would you describe yourself?	_____	_____	_____
How do people treat you?	_____	_____	_____
How did Jesus treat you?	_____	_____	_____
When Jesus met you, what did you and He first talk about?	_____	_____	_____

	NICODEMUS	SAMARITAN WOMAN	ROYAL OFFICIAL
Why were you interested in talking to Jesus about this?	_____	_____	_____
What did Jesus tell you that you needed to do?	_____	_____	_____
Who did you think Jesus was when you first met Him?	_____	_____	_____

Why don't you and your family or friends act this out? Do a little play.

It's a Wrap!

Did you know that Jesus traveled so much? His journey took Him to interesting places where He met many different kinds of people, and He cared about every one of them. Oftentimes kids (and sometimes adults, too) can be mean to others who are different than they are. They can tease them and make others laugh—but their words hurt. Has anyone ever said anything about you that hurt? If so, you understand and won't want to do that to anyone else.

Jesus made a good difference in everyone's life. He told the Samaritan woman about living water, and He healed the royal official's son. And they both came to believe in Him. Isn't that what we want people to do? Believe on Jesus so that they can have eternal life? Of course!

When you talk to people, why don't you pray and ask Jesus to show you what to say to help them believe in Him too? This is called being a good witness. A witness tells what he or she has seen, knows, or believes. We are praying you will be a faithful witness to Jesus.

5

John 5

Sometimes movies take place in the future. Sometimes they take place in the past. Have you ever wanted to travel to a different place in time? Well, you can...sort of. This week we're going to show you how you can travel back to Bible times by looking for clues and asking questions of the passage you're studying. Don't forget to pray before you start this week.

Sneak Peak

First, we'll need to storyboard this chapter. Write out or draw the main events of John 5:

JOHN 5:1-9:   **JOHN 5:10-47:**

Our memory verse for this week is John
5:24. Write it out on a 3 x 5 card and read
to it often during the week so that you've
memorized it by the end of Day Five.

DAY 2

The Great Time Machine

Today is the day we travel back in time. And our time
machine is called *context*. When you study the Bible, it's very
important to understand the *context* of a passage. Context is
the setting in which something is told or found. For instance,

where would you find a bed in your house? What about a refrigerator? A bedroom is the context for a bed. And a kitchen is the context for a refrigerator. When you look at context in the Bible, you look at the verses surrounding the passage you're studying. You think about where the passage fits in the big picture of the whole Bible. Context also includes:

- the place where something happens (Jesus was born in Bethlehem, not New York)

- the time an event occurs (the sun rises in the morning, not in the evening)

- the customs of a group of people (girls wouldn't have been allowed to wear jeans in Bible times)

- the time in history an event occurred (Noah and the ark came before Jonah and the big fish)

Sometimes you can discover all of these things from just the verses you're studying. Sometimes you have to study more passages of Scripture. But it's always important to be on the lookout for context because it helps you discover for yourself what the Bible is saying.

Let's look at the context of John 5:1-29, using the Observation Worksheet for John 5.

First mark the names of the places Jesus went. (Hint: A place doesn't always have to be a country or a city.) Location is very important. It tells you WHERE something happens or WHERE the characters are supposed to be. You can mark the locations by underlining them twice with a green pencil, or you can make up your own way to mark them.

John 5:1

_____

John 5:2

_____

John 5:14

_____

Now let's see WHEN these things happened. You can mark time, like days of the week or special festivals, on your Observation Worksheet by drawing a green clock like this in the margin. You can also put a clock by words like "after," "afterward," "when," and "then." You should find at least three references to time in John 5:1-29. Write the verses below:

John 5:_____
John 5:_____
John 5:_____

These markings will help you see WHEN and WHERE Jesus went and the order in which certain events happened. They will show you what happened on one day, then the next day, then the next. They help you see that Jesus was a real person who lived at a certain time and in a certain place.

In a couple of days, we will learn about one of the customs in John 5 that was really important when Jesus was alive. Remember, this is another way to look at context.

DAY 3

A Big Question

Read John 5:1-18 slowly and carefully. Then answer the following questions. (Remember the 5 W's and an H!)

John 5:1,5,10 WHO are the main people you read about in this passage?

_____

John 5:2 WHERE was Jesus when He did this miracle?

_____

John 5:5 HOW long had the man been sick?

_____

John 5:7 WHAT did the lame man tell Jesus when He asked, "Do you want to get well?"

_____

John 5:8-9 HOW did Jesus help the man?

_____

Here Come the Bad Guys

One thing that makes a movie exciting is when the good guys face off against the bad guys. When the good guys and the bad guys meet, it usually makes us hold our breath, wondering what will happen next. In John's Gospel, chapter 5 tells us about the first face-off between Jesus (the good guy) and the religious leaders (the bad guys). All religious leaders weren't bad, just some. You'll see why they were the bad guys when you read the verses we tell you about next. Let's see how it all happens…

Remember the lame man Jesus healed on the Sabbath in the verses we looked at yesterday? Well, not everyone was happy that Jesus healed him. Read verses 16 to 18 to find out what happened next.

WHO was not happy about this healing?

_____

WHY weren't they happy?

_____

Rules for the Sabbath

The Pharisees made their own laws based on their interpretation of God's Law. These laws, called the *Mishnah,* are not found in the Bible. The Pharisees created very strict rules about the Sabbath. There were 39 different kinds of work that were forbidden on the Sabbath. Here are some other things that you were forbidden to do on the Sabbath:

1. You could not search for fleas in your clothes.
2. You could not read by lamplight.
3. You could not carry your bed.
4. You could not heal anyone.
5. You could not put vinegar on a toothache.

These customs were followed in Bible times. They are part of the *context* of this story. But you won't find too many people following these rules today.

John 5:10 Which Sabbath rule did the man break?

_____

John 5:15-16 Which rule did Jesus break?

_____

Bible Scramble

Unscramble the words to find the missing words of your Bible verse. The mystery word gives you an important clue about why the Jews were angry with Jesus.

John 5:24

"_____, truly, I say to you, he who hears My word,

and _____ _____ who sent Me, has

_____ life, and does not come into judgment,

_____ has _____ out of _____ into life.

1. sadsep   — — ◯ — — — —

2. adeht   — — ◯ — — —

3. eesbeilv   ◯ — — — — — — —

4. ubt   ◯ — —

5. trenlea   — — — — — ◯ —

6. luytr   ◯ — — — —

7. mHi   ◯ — —

Witnesses for the Defense

This week you're going to look for only three key words. We are going to mark "believe," "life" ("eternal life"), and a new key word. That word is "witness." Read John 5:30-47 and mark these words on your Observation Worksheet for this chapter. (If you have time, read through John 5:1-29 and mark every "believe" and "life.")

Some of the Jewish leaders wanted to kill Jesus because He was claiming to be the Son of God (see John 5:18). They didn't believe Him. But Jesus was telling the truth. He even had witnesses. Look where you marked the key word "witness" and list some of them (hint: They're not all people):

John 5:33

_____

John 5:36

_____

John 5:37

_____

John 5:39

_____

It's a Wrap!

We've traveled in time this week using our time machine *context*. We discovered that by looking at where things happened and how they were done, the people in the Bible become more real to us. Wow! Do you realize how much you've learned in these five weeks? Terrific job!

Now let's wrap it up for you.

Has anyone ever asked you to lie? Or worse still, to lie about another person? Or maybe you had a chance to tell the truth about someone, but you didn't because you knew if you did, others wouldn't like you. Were you a true witness or a false witness?

John the Baptist was a true witness—even though many people didn't believe him (John 3:32). Jesus and God were pleased with him, and that is what is important. God always knows whether or not we tell the truth. If you want to be a good witness for Jesus, you'll always tell the truth—just like Jesus did. He was God's faithful witness. You be one too.

6

John 6

Do you like watching mystery movies? A mystery movie is fun because we often don't understand everything right away. Slowly, bit by bit, we begin to figure things out until the moment arrives when it all becomes clear. In many ways Jesus was a mystery to the people around Him. They could sense that He was different, but they couldn't always figure out exactly *why*.

Throughout the Gospel of John, Jesus reveals more and more about Himself as the Jewish leaders, the disciples, and the crowds all ask Him questions about who He is. Let's see what part of the mystery we're going to film this week…

Sneak Peak

Let's create our storyboard by reading through John 6 and identifying the main events:

JOHN 6:1-15:

JOHN 6:16-21:

JOHN 6:22-59:

JOHN 6:60-71:

Now let's write out the memory verse for the week on a 3 x 5 card. The verse is John 6:35. Remember to read it often during the week until you have it memorized.

DAY 2

Lunch Break!

Today's story might make you a little hungry. Even directors need a break so they can eat. Read John 6:1-14 and mark the key word "sign" ("signs"). Also mark locations and words that show time. Don't forget, festivals or feasts tell you what time of year it is because they happen the same time year after year, like Christmas. When you finish, answer these questions.

John 6:5 Jesus asked Philip, "WHERE are we to buy
_____ , that these may eat?"

John 6:6 WHY did Jesus ask Philip this question?

_____

John 6:9 HOW much food did the boy have?

_____

John 6:11-12 HOW did Jesus solve the problem of not having enough food?

_____

John 6:11 WHAT did Jesus do before He gave them the food to eat?

_____

John 6:13 HOW much food was left over after Jesus fed the 5000?

_____

Staying Afloat

Today we're going to film an action scene. Watch for the incredible thing Jesus is going to do when you say "Action!"

Read John 6:15-21. Mark any time phrases or locations.

John 6:15 WHERE did Jesus go to be alone?

_____

John 6:16 WHERE did the disciples go?

_____

John 6:19 HOW does Jesus come to them?

_____

John 6:19 HOW did the disciples respond?

_____

John 6:20 WHAT did Jesus say to them?

_____

Spotlight on Key Words

We're going to look at just one new key word today—well, kind of. Sometimes different words mean the same thing. For example, you can call a movie a "film" or a "picture show" or a "flick." These words are *synonyms!* Our key word today is "bread," but there are many synonyms for the word "bread" in this chapter. Let's find some of them.

John 6:26 l ___ ___ ___ ___ ___

John 6:31 m ___ ___ ___ ___

John 6:31 b___ ___ ___ ___   ___ ___ ___

___ ___ ___ ___ ___ ___ ___ ___

John 6:35 b___ ___ ___ ___   ___ ___

l ___ ___ ___

Now turn to your Observation Worksheet which covers John 6:22-59 and mark the key word "bread" and all its synonyms. Now let's see how our key word helps solve the mystery about who Jesus is.

John 6:33   WHAT did Jesus say the bread of God does?

_____

John 6:35   WHO is the bread of life?

_____

John 6:35   WHAT promise does Jesus give to those who come to Him?

_____

Handling an Unhappy Cast

Today, you're going to go back to your Observation Worksheet for John 6 and mark two other key words, "eternal life" and "believe," in verses 22-59. When you come to verse 59, notice where Jesus is and double underline it. Also mark these words Jesus said: "will raise him up on the last day." This is Jesus' promise to everyone who believes.

List three things you learn from these verses about eternal life.

1. _____

2. _____

3. _____

This isn't the first time Jesus has talked about eternal life. Think back to probably the most famous line that Jesus said. (Hint: It was your memory verse in Week Three.) WHO did Jesus say it to?_____

But there's more! Jesus told someone else about eternal life in John 4:14. WMO was it?_____

If you can imagine this, some people *didn't* like what Jesus had to say. Read John 5:60-71 and mark "disciples." Then find out who was unhappy, how they showed they weren't happy, and why (if it tells you).

John 6:60-61

_____

John 6:64

_____

John 6:66

_____

John 6:70-71 WHO is going to betray Jesus?

_____

John 6:68-69 WHO would not walk away?

_____

It's a Wrap!

This week you learned that Jesus calls Himself the bread of life. Do you wonder why Jesus called Himself bread? Just like the bread you eat at lunch gives you energy for life on earth, so Jesus gives you everything you need for eternal life.

Not everyone will have life in heaven. As you read in John 6:66, even some of Jesus' disciples walked away from Him. They missed eternal life.

Are you going to be a true disciple of Jesus and believe Him no matter what? If you do, you'll have eternal life and will be raised up when you die and go to heaven.

7

John 7

In John 7, the bad guys are starting to get serious. In fact, they want to kill Jesus! All the uproar is about who Jesus really is. Many of the Jewish people are starting to ask, "Is Jesus the Christ, the long-expected Messiah?" "Christ" and "Messiah" are the same (John 1:41). Messiah means "the promised one." From the time people first sinned, God promised He would send a Savior. Many Jews were expecting the Messiah to come and set them free from evil rulers. They didn't really think they needed a Savior to die to take their sins away. They thought they could just be really good, keep the law, and go to heaven.

Did you remember to pray before you started this week?

Sneak Peak

Read the following verses and write out who some people think Jesus might be:

John 7:12 _____

John 7:26 _____

John 7:40 _____

Who do *you* think Jesus is?

_____

The memory verse for this week is actually two verses: John 7:16-17. As usual, it's a good idea to write what you're memorizing on a 3 x 5 card so that you can look at it again and again throughout the week.

Let's create our storyboard for this chapter. Read John 7 carefully, and write out or draw the main events:

JOHN 7:1-13:   **JOHN 1:14-24:**

JOHN 7:25-36:

JOHN 7:37-44:

JOHN 7:45-53:

Mark the words "believe," "Spirit," and "Christ" on your Observation Worksheet for John 7:1-43. Double-underline locations in green and mark time with a clock.

Location, Location, Location!

Every filmmaker looks carefully for the best place to film the picture. This process is called "scouting for locations." Take a few minutes to scout where this story takes place. On the map of the Holy Land below, circle the places mentioned in this chapter.

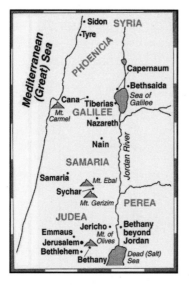

MAP OF
THE
HOLY LAND

John 7:3 WHERE did Jesus' brothers ask Him to go?

_____

John 7:8 Did Jesus go then?

_____

John 7:8 WHY not?

_____

John 7:9 WHAT did He do then? (Did you double underline this location in green?)

_____

Now it's time for a little detective work. Let's see if we can discover the city where the Feast of Booths was held.

Mark 11:11 WHAT important building is located in Jerusalem?

_____

John 7:14 WHO is at the temple?

_____

John 7:2,14 Jesus is at WHAT feast?

_____

WHERE is the Feast of Booths?

_____

WHY HAVE A FEAST OF BOOTHS?

After God led His people out of Egypt, the people had to camp in the wilderness. The first night, they made shelters like our tents. They called these tents "booths." During the Feast of Booths, the people remembered what God did for their ancestors. They thanked God for His loving care and protection while they were wandering in the desert. It is also a time when they gave thanks for the autumn season and its harvest.

Who Am I?

As you are beginning to see, the big debate among the Jewish people was over who Jesus was. For each verse, tell who was speaking and who they thought Jesus was:

	Who Said It	What They Said
John 7:12	_____	_____
John 7:12	_____	_____
John 7:20	_____	_____
John 7:40	_____	_____
John 7:41	_____	_____

People had lots of ideas about who Jesus was. Many of them really wanted to believe He was sent from God. But an argument arose over where the Old Testament said the Christ would be born. Read this prophecy in Micah 5:2. Where was the "ruler of Israel" to be born?_____

People who knew Jesus didn't know He was born in Bethlehem.

John 1:45 WHERE did they think He came from?

_____

Look at your map on page 66. WHAT region is Nazareth in?

_____

John 7:43-45 You can understand why the people were confused. So WHAT did the multitude and chief priests want to do now?

_____

John 7:46 WHAT was the officers' excuse for not bring-ing in Jesus?

_____

John 7:50-51 WHO stood up for Jesus?

_____

It's a Puzzle

Let's see how many of these questions you can answer on your own! Don't look at the Scripture clues unless you have to.

Feast of Booths

Down

1. When Jesus went to the Feast of the Booths, He went in _____. (Hint: It's the same way Nicodemus visited Jesus—John 7:10.)
3. Who was seeking Jesus at the feast? (John 7:1)
6. How does John 7:12 describe the way in which the multitudes were talking about Jesus?
8. Who defended Jesus? (John 7:50)
10. What did the multitudes say Jesus had? (John 7:20)

Across

2. What were the Jews doing when they heard Jesus teach in the Temple courts? (Hint: It means to be amazed.) (John 7:15)

4. Where was Jesus unwilling to walk? (John 7:1-2)
5. What did Jesus' brothers want Jesus' disciples to see? (It's another word for miracles.) (John 7:3)
7. What part of Israel do some of the multitude think Jesus is from? (John 7:41)
9. What family or offspring did some of the multitude know the Christ would come from? (John 7:42)
11. What kind of deeds does Jesus teach about that makes the world hate Him? (John 7:7)
12. Who wasn't believing in Jesus? (John 7:5)

(Answers are on p. 94.)

Make a list of the people in chapter 7 who believed in Jesus and a list of those who did not:

Believed   Did Not Believe

_____   _____

_____   _____

_____   _____

It's Your Turn Now

How are you doing with this week's memory verse? Take a look at John 7:14-17 and see if *you* can make up questions using the 5 W's and an H.

WHO

_____

WHAT

_____

WHEN

_____

WHERE

_____

WHY

_____

HOW

_____

It's a Wrap!

Who is Jesus? That seems to be the question on everyone's mind. Some thought He had a demon. Others thought He was the Christ. But as you learned from the memory verse, if you really want to know who Jesus is, you must be willing to do God's will. Then God will show you the truth.

Do you want to do God's will—to obey Him and believe Him? If you do, then God will always show you what is true. Just ask God to show you—it will please Him very much!

8

John 8

This is a big week for the film crew! We have a lot to do and not a lot of time to do it in. So many big important things happen in John 8 that we can't skip anything.

Sneak Peak

So we can see where we're headed this week, let's create our storyboard. Read the chapter, then draw a picture or briefly describe the main action for each section.

JOHN 8:1-11:

JOHN 8:12-20:

JOHN 8:21-30:

JOHN 8:31-59:

What are the names given for Jesus in this chapter? List them below.

John 8:1

_____

John 8:4

_____

John 8:11

_____

John 8:12

_____

John 8:28

_____

John 8:36

_____

John 8:58 (Hint: Look up Exodus 3:14.)

_____

This week's memory verse is John 8:32.
Write it on a 3 x 5 card and review it
throughout the week.

Spotlight on Key Words

Today we're going to mark the key words "witness" ("bears witness"), "believe," "truth" and its synonym "truly, truly" (which means "I tell you the truth"), and a brand-new key word, "sin" ("sins"). You may want to color "sin" brown, because brown is the color of dirt, and sin makes us dirty.

One day a woman caught in sin (there's the word "sin" that you marked) was brought before Jesus. The scribes and Pharisees said that the law of Moses commanded that the woman be stoned. They wanted to know what Jesus would do. They wanted to test Him. But Jesus did something that was very surprising. On your Observation Worksheet for Chapter 8 (on page 119), read verses 1-11.

John 8:6 WHY did the scribes and Pharisees want to test Jesus?

_____

John 8:6 WHAT did Jesus do?

_____

John 8:7 HOW did Jesus answer the Pharisees?

_____

John 8:9 WHAT did the Pharisees do in answer to Jesus' instructions, beginning with the oldest?

_____

John 8:10-11 Were there any scribes or Pharisees left who could throw the first stone?

_____

John 8:11 Jesus could have thrown the first stone because He had no sin, but He didn't. Instead, WHAT did He say to the woman?

_____

White Hats and Black Hats

Contrasts

In old western movies, everybody knew that good cowboys wore white hats, and bad cowboys wore black hats. Do you notice how white and black are opposite and good and bad are opposite? We can say that white and black are *contrasts*. And good and bad are contrasts. A contrast shows how things are different or opposite. The Bible uses many contrasts, such as *light* and *dark* or *truth* and *lie*.

Now look at the contrast in John 8:12. Who does Jesus say He is?

_____

What two things are opposites in this verse?

_____

Jesus points out several contrasts between the Pharisees and Himself. In the following chart, write out the things He says about Himself and the things He says about the Pharisees:

John 8:14

Jesus_____

Pharisees_____

John 8:15

Jesus_____

Pharisees_____

John 8:23 (Hint: There are two contrasts in this verse.)

Jesus_____

Pharisees_____

In these verses you've seen how Jesus was different from the religious leaders who were against Him. Good for you! You know so much more about Jesus now than you did before. Look at all you have learned just by studying God's Word for yourself. We are sooooo proud of you! We pray that you'll get many of your friends to study the Bible like this.

To Tell the Truth

Now let's look at two verses that use our key word "truth" a lot. In John 8:31-32, Jesus speaks "to those Jews who had believed in Him." List the three things that will happen if a person "abides," which means "stays," in His Word.

Jesus said, "If you abide in My Word," then:

1. _____

2. _____

3. _____

John 8:40 WHERE did Jesus' truth come from?

_____

John 8:44 WHY does Jesus say we shouldn't believe what the devil says?

_____

We've just seen an important contrast.

God is the t ___ ___ ___ ___ . The devil is a l ___ ___ ___ .

DAY 5

There's Something About That Name

Today we'll look at one of the most amazing statements Jesus makes about Himself. Several times in this chapter Jesus calls Himself "I AM." Read verses 24, 28, and 58, then fill in the blanks.

John 8:24 Unless you believe _____, you
_____.

John 8:28 When you _____,
then you will know _____.

John 8:58 Before Abraham was born, _____.

If you were making a movie, you would want to make sure you had all your facts straight. You might check other books or ask people who knew the answers. When you're studying the Bible, you can always use other parts of the Bible to double-check your facts because all of God's Word is true.

We're going to use another part of the Bible to check out what John 8 says about the words "I AM."

I AM seems like an unusual name for someone to have. But it's the name God gave Himself, so we should pay attention. It was a holy name, so holy that the Jewish people couldn't even say it aloud. Read Exodus 3:10-14, where God told Moses to lead the Israelites out of Egypt.

According to Exodus 3:14, when the name I AM is used, whose name is it?

_____

WHAT does Jesus say in John 8:58?

_____

When Jesus called Himself I AM, WHO was He claiming to be?

_____

If anyone ever called himself God, or used God's name as his own name, or said that he was equal with God, that person would be committing a very serious act, called "blasphemy."

According to Jewish law, the punishment for blasphemy was death. The people were told to stone the one who blasphemed—to throw rocks at him until he died.

Why do you think the Jews pick up stones to throw at Jesus in verse 59?

_____

Is Jesus God? Do you remember the very first verse of John's Gospel? Read John 1:1 and write out who the Word is.

_____

Were the Jews wrong to stone Jesus? WHY?

_____

Can Jesus lie?

_____

Now read John 1:14. WHO is the Word?

_____

Finally read John 8:24. WHAT will happen to those who don't believe Jesus is God?

_____

It's a Wrap!

The fact that Jesus was telling the truth about being God makes Him the most unique person who ever lived. He was a man, and He was God. Do you believe Jesus is God? The devil doesn't want you to believe this. He doesn't want you to get close to God—ever. But when you believe Jesus is God, and you receive Jesus as your Savior, then you become a child of God. People change when they become part of God's family. Because the Holy Spirit lives in every true child of God, they are able to say no to sin. As John 8:34-36 says, a child of God is no longer a slave of sin because Jesus sets him free from being sin's slave. A child of God wants to obey God.

In the space below, write out a short prayer. Tell God what you believe about Him. Next to it, put down today's date

Date: _____

_____

_____

_____

_____

_____

_____

_____

_____

9

John 9 and 10

Can you imagine never, ever, *ever* being able to see? Not your parents, not your dog, not the blue sky and sun—nothing! And then one day, you meet a man and He gives you your sight? What would that be like? How would you feel? Wouldn't that be *awesome!*

That's what Jesus does in John 9. And guess who got mad again? The Pharisees! This chapter is like a trial from one of those old lawyer movies—only this time Jesus is on trial and the Pharisees are the prosecutors!

As you begin your lesson, don't forget to pray and ask God to help you understand His book, the Bible.

Sneak Peak

This week we're going to cover two chapters instead of one, so we'll just storyboard the highlights in each chapter. We'll do John 9:1-14 first.

JOHN 9:1-14:

_____

In John 9, mark these keywords:

blind

sinned

sight

Watch for these words as we see what Jesus is going to do.

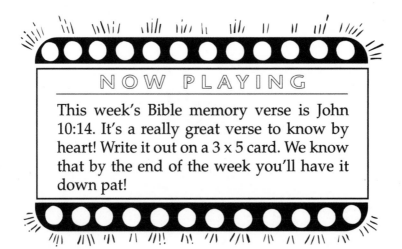

NOW PLAYING

This week's Bible memory verse is John 10:14. It's a really great verse to know by heart! Write it out on a 3 x 5 card. We know that by the end of the week you'll have it down pat!

The Light Dawns

John 9:2 WHAT is the question that the disciples have for Jesus?

_____

John 9:3 WHAT is His answer?

_____

As you read through this chapter, watch the change in the blind man's understanding of who Jesus is. Read each of the five verses below, and then write down what the blind man says about Jesus in each of them:

John 9:11 _____

John 9:17 _____

John 9:25 _____

John 9:33 _____

John 9:38 _____

Read John 9:13-34. Imagine that you are a court reporter, a person who writes down what is said at a trial. Make a list of the questions the religious leaders ask, and then write out how the formerly blind man or others answer them. Put down who answers the question. It might be even more interesting if you acted out the parts after you write them down. Get a table and make it the judge's bench. Then set a chair next to it as the witness stand.

John 9:15   Question:_____

                   Answer:_____

John 9:17   Question:_____

                   Answer:_____

John 9:19-21   Question:_____

                   Answer:_____

John 9:24-27   Question:_____

                   Answer:_____

Now it's Jesus' turn to ask a question.

John 9:35 WHAT does Jesus ask the man?

_____

John 9:36-38 HOW does the man respond to Jesus?

_____

This is another of the signs (miracles) Jesus did so we might believe in Him (John 20:30-31). Mark the word "signs" in John 9:16.

Wild and Wooly

Now let's turn our attention to chapter 10. This is where the animal stars come in. In some movies, animals act like people. Here we're going to see how people are like animals. In this chapter we learn about Jesus as the Good Shepherd. Let's storyboard John 10:1-15.

JOHN 10:1-15:

_____

In John 10, mark "shepherd" with a 🪝 and "sheep" with a 🐑 .

The Pharisees threw the man who had been blind out of the synagogue. They didn't care about the man. But Jesus was different. In the next verses, He shows how he cares for people like the man who was blind.

Read John 10:1-28. See if you can find the verses where Jesus talks about being a shepherd and write them down.

"I am the good shepherd." _____

"I am the door of the sheep."_____
(For more on this, read the Sheep Facts that follow.)

John 10:11 WHAT does the good shepherd do?

_____

In the Bible, people are sometimes described as sheep. Look up the verses below and write down the part that mentions people as sheep or what God will do for His sheep.

Ezekiel 34:11 _____

Ezekiel 34:31_____

Psalm 95:7_____

Psalm 100:3 _____

Isaiah 53:6 _____

Like the sheep you read about in Isaiah, we often want to go our own way. We need our Shepherd (Jesus) to show us the way.

Here are some more fun facts about sheep. See if these fluffly little animals are always as cute as they look!

Sheep Facts

1. Sheep get scared very easily.
2. Sheep give in to peer pressure. They do what all the other sheep are doing! If one sheep gets scared and runs, all the others run with it.
3. Sheep are very stubborn. They need a shepherd to guide them.
4. Sheep are dumb animals. Sometimes they won't even try to run to safety if there is danger around. They will just freeze and not even cry out.

5. Sheep have a "butting order." If a younger sheep is eating in a patch of grass the older sheep wants, the older one will butt the younger one out of the way! But when the shepherd comes, they all behave themselves.

6. Have you ever had a bug get up your nose? It happens to sheep all the time. And sometimes the flies or gnats lay eggs in there. When the eggs hatch, the growing larvae irritate the sheep's nose. Some sheep beat their heads against trees or rocks to try to get these pests to stop bothering them. When the good shepherd sees this happening to a sheep, he puts some oil on the sheep's head and around its nose to kill the bugs.

7. Sheep can become "cast down." They get turned over on their backs and can die if the shepherd doesn't turn them right side up quickly. A sheep becomes "cast down" because he's looking for a soft spot, or he has too much wool, or he's just too fat!

8. In the sheepfold—the place where the sheep sleep— the shepherd will lie down in the opening and be the door. If a thief or robber or an animal tries to get in and hurt the sheep, they have to cross over the shepherd.

Spotlight on Key Words

Turn to your Observation Worksheet for Chapter 10, read verses 1-30. Mark the words listed below:

Thief (Robber)

The information in "Sheep Facts" was gathered from Philip Keller's book *A Shepherd Looks at Psalm 23.*

Door

Truly, truly (when you see these words, circle them)

Whenever Jesus says "truly, truly" you know that He is going to say something very important. Write out below the verses where you circled "truly, truly" on your Observation Worksheet (don't forget to include the reference!):

1. _____

2. _____

Jesus says, "I am the ___ ___ ___ r" twice in chapter ten.

You can find the answer in verses _____ and _____.

Jesus also says, "I am the good

___ ___ ___ p ___ ___ ___ ___."

You can find the answer in verses _____ and _____.

John 10:4-5 HOW can you tell if a sheep belongs to a certain shepherd?

_____

Whose sheep are you?

_____

When you belong to God's sheepfold, you'll never be alone. Friends may kick you out of their group because you won't do sinful things like they do. But you will always be God's own sheep, and no one can ever, *ever* take you away from God. He will care for you as your Shepherd.

Read John 10:10 and 10:27-30 again. Thank God that Jesus as a Shepherd laid down His life for you so you could have life. Remember, this is better than being part of a group of friends who don't follow Shepherd Jesus.

You've Done It!

Today is the *last* day of the *last* lesson in this book. Look how much you've learned! Look at all you've done! You know enough about Jesus now to make the first part of your movie about Him! It's time for a quiz about your movie. See how many questions you can answer before you look up the verses.

John 20:30-31 WHAT was John's purpose or reason for writing this Gospel?

_____

John 2:23 WHY did Jesus do signs?

_____

Can you remember the signs Jesus did? Think hard! We'll give you a hint, so try getting the answer before you look up the verses.

John 2:6-10 _____
(Hint: Stone pots were involved.)

John 4:46-54 _____
(Hint: Jesus didn't even meet the person he healed.)

John 5:1-9 _____
(Hint: This happened to a man who had been sick for 38 years.)

John 6:1-14 _____
(Hint: This miracle might make you hungry!)

John 9:1-16 _____
(Hint: Jesus had to spit to help this man.)

Jesus tells us a lot about Himself. Can you fill in the "I am" statements below?

John 6:48 "I am _____."

John 8:12 "I am _____."

John 10:7 "I am _____."

John 10:14 "I am _____."

In the beginning of the movie we talked about all the people we would meet. See how many of them you can remember.

John 1:6   J ___ ___ ___

John 1:40 A ___ ___ ___ ___ ___   and   S ___ ___ ___ ___

John 1:45 P ___ ___ ___ ___ ___   and

           N ___ ___ ___ ___ ___ ___ ___ ___

John 3:1   N ___ ___ ___ ___ ___ ___ ___ ___

John 4:1   P ___ ___ ___ ___ ___ ___ ___ ___

John 4:7   W___ ___ ___ ___   ___ ___

         S___ ___ ___ ___ ___ ___

John 4:46 R __ __ __ __   O __ __ __ __ __ __ __

John 6:9 L __ __

John 8:3 W __ __ __ __   C __ __ __ __ __

        I __   A __ __ __ __ __ __ __

John 9:1 B __ __ __ __   M __ __

It's a Wrap!

You've done a great job! You worked so hard. You now know a lot about how to study the Bible for yourself...inductively! You've learned how to ask questions using the 5 W's and an H. You've learned big ideas like *synonyms, context,* and *contrast.* Best of all, you've learned more about the important things Jesus taught. And *that's* why we study the Bible.

We are sooooo proud of you! You have finished the first part of your movie. Don't forget to fill out and send us the card in the back of this book. We have something special to send to you! The next book in this series is part two of your film. It's called *Awesome Love, Awesome Power.* Do you know about the awesome love God has for you and the awesome power He wants to give you? That's what you'll see next on the screen of God's Word. You don't want to miss it!

Puzzle Answers

Page 34

Across:
2 BELIEVES
3 WRATH OF GOD
7 JUDGED
8 HEAVEN
4 PERISH

Down clues visible in grid:
6 GOD IS TRUE
1 ETERNAL LIFE
5 NT JUDGED

Crossword Fun

Page 43

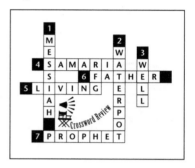

4 SAMARIA
6 FATHER
5 LIVING
7 PROPHET
1 MESSIAH
2 WELL
3 WELL

Crossword Review

Page 70

2 MARVELING
4 JUDEA
5 WORKS
7 GALILEE
9 DAVID
11 EVIL
12 BROTHERS
1 SCRET
3 JEWS
6 GRUMBLING
8 NICODEMUS
10 DEMON

Feast of Booths

The Gospel of John

Chapter 1

1 In the beginning was the Word, and the Word was with God, and the Word was God.

2 He was in the beginning with God.

3 All things came into being by Him, and apart from Him nothing came into being that has come into being.

4 In Him was life, and the life was the light of men.

5 And the light shines in the darkness, and the darkness did not comprehend it.

6 There came a man, sent from God, whose name was John.

7 He came for a witness, that he might bear witness of the light, that all might believe through him.

8 He was not the light, but came that he might bear witness of the light.

9 There was the true light which, coming into the world, enlightens every man.

10 He was in the world, and the world was made through Him, and the world did not know Him.

11 He came to His own, and those who were His own did not receive Him.

12 But as many as received Him, to them He gave the right to become children of God, even to those who believe in His name,

13 who were born not of blood, nor of the will of the flesh, nor of the will of man, but of God.

14 And the Word became flesh, and dwelt among us, and we beheld His glory, glory as of the only begotten from the Father, full of grace and truth.

15 John bore witness of Him, and cried out, saying, "This was He of whom I said, 'He who comes after me has a higher rank than I, for He existed before me.'"

16 For of His fulness we have all received, and grace upon grace.

17 For the Law was given through Moses; grace and truth were realized through Jesus Christ.

18 No man has seen God at any time; the only begotten God, who is in the bosom of the Father, He has explained Him.

19 And this is the witness of John, when the Jews sent to him priests and Levites from Jerusalem to ask him, "Who are you?"

20 And he confessed, and did not deny, and he confessed, "I am not the Christ."

21 And they asked him, "What then? Are you Elijah?" And he said, "I am not." "Are you the Prophet?" And he answered, "No."

22 They said then to him, "Who are you, so that we may give an answer to those who sent us? What do you say about yourself?"

23 He said, "I am A VOICE OF ONE CRYING IN THE WILDERNESS, 'MAKE STRAIGHT THE WAY OF THE LORD,' as Isaiah the prophet said."

24 Now they had been sent from the Pharisees.

25 And they asked him, and said to him, "Why then are you baptizing, if you are not the Christ, nor Elijah, nor the Prophet?"

26 John answered them saying, "I baptize in water, but among you stands One whom you do not know.

27 "It is He who comes after me, the thong of whose sandal I am not worthy to untie."

28 These things took place in Bethany beyond the Jordan, where John was baptizing.

29 The next day he saw Jesus coming to him, and said, "Behold, the Lamb of God who takes away the sin of the world!

30 "This is He on behalf of whom I said, 'After me comes a Man who has a higher rank than I, for He existed before me.'

31 "And I did not recognize Him, but in order that He might be manifested to Israel, I came baptizing in water."

32 And John bore witness saying, "I have beheld the Spirit descending as a dove out of heaven, and He remained upon Him.

33 "And I did not recognize Him, but He who sent me to baptize in water said to me, 'He upon whom you see the Spirit descending and remaining upon Him, this is the one who baptizes in the Holy Spirit.'

34 "And I have seen, and have borne witness that this is the Son of God."

35 Again the next day John was standing with two of his disciples,

36 and he looked upon Jesus as He walked, and said, "Behold, the Lamb of God!"

37 And the two disciples heard him speak, and they followed Jesus.

38 And Jesus turned, and beheld them following, and said to them, "What do you seek?" And they said to Him, " Rabbi (which translated means Teacher), where are You staying?"

39 He said to them, "Come, and you will see." They came therefore and saw where He was staying; and they stayed with Him that day, for it was about the tenth hour.

40 One of the two who heard John speak, and followed Him, was Andrew, Simon Peter's brother.

41 He found first his own brother Simon, and said to him, "We have found the Messiah" (which translated means Christ).

42 He brought him to Jesus. Jesus looked at him, and said, "You are Simon the son of John; you shall be called Cephas" (which is translated Peter).

43 The next day He purposed to go forth into Galilee, and He found Philip. And Jesus said to him, "Follow Me."

44 Now Philip was from Bethsaida, of the city of Andrew and Peter.

45 Philip found Nathanael and said to him, "We have found Him of whom Moses in the Law and also the Prophets wrote, Jesus of Nazareth, the son of Joseph."

46 And Nathanael said to him, "Can any good thing come out of Nazareth?" Philip said to him, "Come and see."

47 Jesus saw Nathanael coming to Him, and *said of him, "Behold, an Israelite indeed, in whom is no guile!"

48 Nathanael said to Him, "How do You know me?" Jesus answered and said to him, "Before Philip called you, when you were under the fig tree, I saw you."

49 Nathanael answered Him, "Rabbi, You are the Son of God; You are the King of Israel."

50 Jesus answered and said to him, "Because I said to you that I saw you under the fig tree, do you believe? You shall see greater things than these."

51 And He said to him, "Truly, truly, I say to you, you shall see the heavens opened, and the angels of God ascending and descending on the Son of Man."

Chapter 2

1 And on the third day there was a wedding in Cana of Galilee, and the mother of Jesus was there;

2 and Jesus also was invited, and His disciples, to the wedding.

3 And when the wine gave out, the mother of Jesus said to Him, "They have no wine."

4 And Jesus said to her, "Woman, what do I have to do with you? My hour has not yet come."

5 His mother said to the servants, "Whatever He says to you, do it."

6 Now there were six stone waterpots set there for the Jewish custom of purification, containing twenty or thirty gallons each.

7 Jesus said to them, "Fill the waterpots with water." And they filled them up to the brim.

8 And He said to them, "Draw some out now, and take it to the headwaiter." And they took it to him.

9 And when the headwaiter tasted the water which had become wine, and did not know where it came from (but the servants who had drawn the water knew), the headwaiter called the bridegroom,

10 and said to him, "Every man serves the good wine first, and when men have drunk freely, then that which is poorer; you have kept the good wine until now."

11 This beginning of His signs Jesus did in Cana of Galilee, and manifested His glory, and His disciples believed in Him.

12 After this He went down to Capernaum, He and His mother, and His brothers, and His disciples; and there they stayed a few days.

13 And the Passover of the Jews was at hand, and Jesus went up to Jerusalem.

14 And He found in the temple those who were selling oxen and sheep and doves, and the moneychangers seated.

15 And He made a scourge of cords, and drove them all out of the temple, with the sheep and the oxen; and He poured out the coins of the moneychangers, and overturned their tables;

16 and to those who were selling the doves He said, "Take these things away; stop making My Father's house a house of merchandise."

17 His disciples remembered that it was written, "ZEAL FOR THY HOUSE WILL CONSUME ME."

18 The Jews therefore answered and said to Him, "What sign do You show to us, seeing that You do these things?"

19 Jesus answered and said to them, "Destroy this temple, and in three days I will raise it up."

20 The Jews therefore said, "It took forty-six years to build this temple, and will You raise it up in three days?"

21 But He was speaking of the temple of His body.

22 When therefore He was raised from the dead, His disciples remembered that He said this; and they believed the Scripture, and the word which Jesus had spoken.

23 Now when He was in Jerusalem at the Passover, during the feast, many believed in His name, beholding His signs which He was doing.

24 But Jesus, on His part, was not entrusting Himself to them, for He knew all men,

25 and because He did not need anyone to bear witness concerning man for He Himself knew what was in man.

Chapter 3

1 Now there was a man of the Pharisees, named Nicodemus, a ruler of the Jews;

2 this man came to Him by night, and said to Him, "Rabbi, we know that You have come from God as a teacher; for no one can do these signs that You do unless God is with him."

3 Jesus answered and said to him, "Truly, truly, I say to you, unless one is born again, he cannot see the kingdom of God."

4 Nicodemus said to Him, "How can a man be born when he is old? He cannot enter a second time into his mother's womb and be born, can he?"

5 Jesus answered, "Truly, truly, I say to you, unless one is born of water and the Spirit, he cannot enter into the kingdom of God.

6 "That which is born of the flesh is flesh, and that which is born of the Spirit is spirit.

7 "Do not marvel that I said to you, 'You must be born again.'

8 "The wind blows where it wishes and you hear the sound of it, but do not know where it comes from and where it is going; so is everyone who is born of the Spirit."

9 Nicodemus answered and said to Him, "How can these things be?"

10 Jesus answered and said to him, "Are you the teacher of Israel, and do not understand these things?

11 "Truly, truly, I say to you, we speak that which we know, and bear witness of that which we have seen; and you do not receive our witness.

12 "If I told you earthly things and you do not believe, how shall you believe if I tell you heavenly things?

13 "And no one has ascended into heaven, but He who descended from heaven, even the Son of Man.

14 "And as Moses lifted up the serpent in the wilderness, even so must the Son of Man be lifted up;

15 that whoever believes may in Him have eternal life.

16 "For God so loved the world, that He gave His only begotten Son, that whoever believes in Him should not perish, but have eternal life.

17 "For God did not send the Son into the world to judge the world, but that the world should be saved through Him.

18 "He who believes in Him is not judged; he who does not believe has been judged already, because he has not believed in the name of the only begotten Son of God.

19 "And this is the judgment, that the light is come into the world, and men loved the darkness rather than the light; for their deeds were evil.

20 "For everyone who does evil hates the light, and does not come to the light, lest his deeds should be exposed.

21 "But he who practices the truth comes to the light, that his deeds may be manifested as having been wrought in God."

22 After these things Jesus and His disciples came into the land of Judea, and there He was spending time with them and baptizing.

23 And John also was baptizing in Aenon near Salim, because there was much water there; and they were coming and were being baptized.

24 For John had not yet been thrown into prison.

25 There arose therefore a discussion on the part of John's disciples with a Jew about purification.

26 And they came to John and said to him, "Rabbi, He who was with you beyond the Jordan, to whom you have borne witness, behold, He is baptizing, and all are coming to Him."

27 John answered and said, "A man can receive nothing, unless it has been given him from heaven.

28 "You yourselves bear me witness, that I said, 'I am not the Christ,' but, 'I have been sent before Him.'

29 "He who has the bride is the bridegroom; but the friend of the bridegroom, who stands and hears him, rejoices greatly because of the bridegroom's voice. And so this joy of mine has been made full.

30 "He must increase, but I must decrease.

31 "He who comes from above is above all, he who is of the earth is from the earth and speaks of the earth. He who comes from heaven is above all.

32 "What He has seen and heard, of that He bears witness; and no man receives His witness.

33 "He who has received His witness has set his seal to this, that God is true.

34 "For He whom God has sent speaks the words of God; for He gives the Spirit without measure.

35 "The Father loves the Son, and has given all things into His hand.

36 "He who believes in the Son has eternal life; but he who does not obey the Son shall not see life, but the wrath of God abides on him."

Chapter 4

1 When therefore the Lord knew that the Pharisees had heard that Jesus was making and baptizing more disciples than John

2 (although Jesus Himself was not baptizing, but His disciples were),

3 He left Judea, and departed again into Galilee.

4 And He had to pass through Samaria.

5 So He came to a city of Samaria, called Sychar, near the parcel of ground that Jacob gave to his son Joseph;

6 and Jacob's well was there. Jesus therefore, being wearied from His journey, was sitting thus by the well. It was about the sixth hour.

7 There came a woman of Samaria to draw water. Jesus said to her, "Give Me a drink."

8 For His disciples had gone away into the city to buy food.

9 The Samaritan woman therefore said to Him, "How is it that You, being a Jew, ask me for a drink since I am a Samaritan woman?" (For Jews have no dealings with Samaritans.)

10 Jesus answered and said to her, "If you knew the gift of God, and who it is who says to you, 'Give Me a drink,' you would have asked Him, and He would have given you living water."

11 She said to Him, "Sir, You have nothing to draw with and the well is deep; where then do You get that living water?

12 "You are not greater than our father Jacob, are You, who gave us the well, and drank of it himself, and his sons, and his cattle?"

13 Jesus answered and said to her, "Everyone who drinks of this water shall thirst again;

14 but whoever drinks of the water that I shall give him shall never thirst; but the water that I shall give him shall become in him a well of water springing up to eternal life."

15 The woman said to Him, "Sir, give me this water, so I will not be thirsty, nor come all the way here to draw."

16 He said to her, "Go, call your husband, and come here."

17 The woman answered and said, "I have no husband." Jesus said to her, "You have well said, 'I have no husband';

18 for you have had five husbands, and the one whom you now have is not your husband; this you have said truly."

19 The woman Said to Him, "Sir, I perceive that You are a prophet.

20 " Our fathers worshiped in this mountain, and you people say that in Jerusalem is the place where men ought to worship."

21 Jesus said to her, "Woman, believe Me, an hour is coming when neither in this mountain, nor in Jerusalem, shall you worship the Father.

22 "You worship that which you do not know; we worship that which we know, for salvation is from the Jews.

23 "But an hour is coming, and now is, when the true worshipers shall worship the Father in spirit and truth; for such people the Father seeks to be His worshipers.

24 "God is spirit, and those who worship Him must worship in spirit and truth."

25 The woman said to Him, "I know that Messiah is coming (He who is called Christ); when that One comes, He will declare all things to us."

26 Jesus said to her, "I who speak to you am He."

27 And at this point His disciples came, and they marveled that He had been speaking with a woman; yet no one said, "What do You seek?" or, "Why do You speak with her?"

28 So the woman left her waterpot, and went into the city, and said to the men,

29 "Come, see a man who told me all the things that I have done; this is not the Christ, is it?"

30 They went out of the city, and were coming to Him.

31 In the meanwhile the disciples were requesting Him, saying, "Rabbi, eat."

32 But He said to them, "I have food to eat that you do not know about."

33 The disciples therefore were saying to one another, "No one brought Him anything to eat, did he?"

34 Jesus said to them, "My food is to do the will of Him who sent Me, and to accomplish His work.

35 "Do you not say, 'There are yet four months, and then comes the harvest'? Behold, I say to you, lift up your eyes, and look on the fields, that they are white for harvest.

36 "Already he who reaps is receiving wages, and is gathering fruit for life eternal; that he who sows and he who reaps may rejoice together.

37 "For in this case the saying is true, 'One sows, and another reaps.'

38 "I sent you to reap that for which you have not labored; others have labored, and you have entered into their labor."

39 And from that city many of the Samaritans believed in Him because of the word of the woman who testified, "He told me all the things that I have done."

40 So when the Samaritans came to Him, they were asking Him to stay with them; and He stayed there two days.

41 And many more believed because of His word;

42 and they were saying to the woman, "It is no longer because of what you said that we believe, for we have heard for ourselves and know that this One is indeed the Savior of the world."

43 And after the two days He went forth from there into Galilee.

44 For Jesus Himself testified that a prophet has no honor in his own country.

45 So when He came to Galilee, the Galileans received Him, having seen all the things that He did in Jerusalem at the feast; for they themselves also went to the feast.

46 He came therefore again to Cana of Galilee where He had made the water wine. And there was a certain royal official, whose son was sick at Capernaum.

47 When he heard that Jesus had come out of Judea into Galilee, he went to Him, and was requesting Him to come down and heal his son; for he was at the point of death.

48 Jesus therefore said to him, "Unless you people see signs and wonders, you simply will not believe."

49 The royal official said to Him, "Sir, come down before my child dies."

50 Jesus said to him, "Go your way; your son lives." The man believed the word that Jesus spoke to him, and he started off.

51 And as he was now going down, his slaves met him, saying that his son was living.

52 So he inquired of them the hour when he began to get better. They said therefore to him, "Yesterday at the seventh hour the fever left him."

53 So the father knew that it was at that hour in which Jesus said to him, "Your son lives"; and he himself believed, and his whole household.

54 This is again a second sign that Jesus performed, when He had come out of Judea into Galilee.

Chapter 5

1 After these things there was a feast of the Jews, and Jesus went up to Jerusalem.

2 Now there is in Jerusalem by the sheep gate a pool, which is called in Hebrew Bethesda, having five porticoes.

3 In these lay a multitude of those who were sick, blind, lame, and withered, [waiting for the moving of the waters;

4 for an angel of the Lord went down at certain seasons into the pool, and stirred up the water; whoever then first, after the stirring up of the water, stepped in was made well from whatever disease with which he was afflicted.]

5 And a certain man was there, who had been thirty-eight years in his sickness.

6 When Jesus saw him lying there, and knew that he had already been a long time in that condition, He said to him, "Do you wish to get well?"

7 The sick man answered Him, "Sir, I have no man to put me into the pool when the water is stirred up, but while I am coming, another steps down before me."

8 Jesus said to him, "Arise, take up your pallet, and walk."

9 And immediately the man became well, and took up his pallet and began to walk.

Now it was the Sabbath on that day.

10 Therefore the Jews were saying to him who was cured, "It is the Sabbath, and it is not permissible for you to carry your pallet."

11 But he answered them, "He who made me well was the one who said to me, 'Take up your pallet and walk.'"

12 They asked him, "Who is the man who said to you, 'Take up your pallet, and walk'?"

13 But he who was healed did not know who it was; for Jesus had slipped away while there was a crowd in that place.

14 Afterward Jesus found him in the temple, and said to him, "Behold, you have become well; do not sin anymore, so that nothing worse may befall you."

15 The man went away, and told the Jews that it was Jesus who had made him well.

16 And for this reason the Jews were persecuting Jesus, because He was doing these things on the Sabbath.

17 But He answered them, "My Father is working until now, and I Myself am working."

18 For this cause therefore the Jews were seeking all the more to kill Him, because He not only was breaking the Sabbath, but also was calling God His own Father, making Himself equal with God.

19 Jesus therefore answered and was saying to them, "Truly, truly, I say to you, the Son can do nothing of Himself, unless it is something He sees the Father doing; for whatever the Father does, these things the Son also does in like manner.

20 "For the Father loves the Son, and shows Him all things that He Himself is doing; and greater works than these will He show Him, that you may marvel.

21 "For just as the Father raises the dead and gives them life, even so the Son also gives life to whom He wishes.

22 "For not even the Father judges anyone, but He has given all judgment to the Son,

23 in order that all may honor the Son, even as they honor the Father. He who does not honor the Son does not honor the Father who sent Him.

24 "Truly, truly, I say to you, he who hears My word, and believes Him who sent Me, has eternal life, and does not come into judgment, but has passed out of death into life.

25 "Truly, truly, I say to you, an hour is coming and now is, when the dead shall hear the voice of the Son of God; and those who hear shall live.

26 "For just as the Father has life in Himself, even so He gave to the Son also to have life in Himself;

27 and He gave Him authority to execute judgment, because He is the Son of Man.

28 "Do not marvel at this; for an hour is coming, in which all who are in the tombs shall hear His voice,

29 and shall come forth; those who did the good deeds to a resurrection of life, those who committed the evil deeds to a resurrection of judgment.

30 "I can do nothing on My own initiative. As I hear, I judge; and My judgment is just, because I do not seek My own will, but the will of Him who sent Me.

31 " If I alone bear witness of Myself, My testimony is not true.

32 "There is another who bears witness of Me, and I know that the testimony which He bears of Me is true.

33 "You have sent to John, and he has borne witness to the truth.

34 "But the witness which I receive is not from man, but I say these things that you may be saved.

35 "He was the lamp that was burning and was shining and you were willing to rejoice for a while in his light.

36 "But the witness which I have is greater than that of John; for the works which the Father has given Me to accomplish, the very works that I do, bear witness of Me, that the Father has sent Me.

37 "And the Father who sent Me, He has borne witness of Me. You have neither heard His voice at any time, nor seen His form.

38 "And you do not have His word abiding in you, for you do not believe Him whom He sent.

39 "You search the Scriptures, because you think that in them you have eternal life; and it is these that bear witness of Me;

40 and you are unwilling to come to Me, that you may have life.

41 "I do not receive glory from men;

42 but I know you, that you do not have the love of God in yourselves.

43 "I have come in My Father's name, and you do not receive Me; if another shall come in his own name, you will receive him.

44 "How can you believe, when you receive glory from one another, and you do not seek the glory that is from the one and only God?

45 "Do not think that I will accuse you before the Father; the one who accuses you is Moses, in whom you have set your hope.

46 "For if you believed Moses, you would believe Me; for he wrote of Me.

47 "But if you do not believe his writings, how will you believe My words?"

Chapter 6

1 After these things Jesus went away to the other side of the Sea of Galilee (or Tiberias).

2 And a great multitude was following Him, because they were seeing the signs which He was performing on those who were sick.

3 And Jesus went up on the mountain, and there He sat with His disciples.

4 Now the Passover, the feast of the Jews, was at hand.

5 Jesus therefore lifting up His eyes, and seeing that a great multitude was coming to Him, said to Philip, "Where are we to buy bread, that these may eat?"

6 And this He was saying to test him; for He Himself knew what He was intending to do.

7 Philip answered Him, "Two hundred denarii worth of bread is not sufficient for them, for everyone to receive a little."

8 One of His disciples, Andrew, Simon Peter's brother, said to Him,

9 "There is a lad here who has five barley loaves and two fish, but what are these for so many people?"

10 Jesus said, "Have the people sit down." Now there was much grass in the place. So the men sat down, in number about five thousand.

11 Jesus therefore took the loaves; and having given thanks, He distributed to those who were seated; likewise also of the fish as much as they wanted.

12 And when they were filled, He said to His disciples, "Gather up the leftover fragments that nothing may be lost."

13 And so they gathered them up, and filled twelve baskets with fragments from the five barley loaves, which were left over by those who had eaten.

14 When therefore the people saw the sign which He had performed, they said, "This is of a truth the Prophet who is to come into the world."

15 Jesus therefore perceiving that they were intending to come and take Him by force, to make Him king, withdrew again to the mountain by Himself alone.

16 Now when evening came, His disciples went down to the sea,

17 and after getting into a boat, they started to cross the sea to Capernaum. And it had already become dark, and Jesus had not yet come to them.

18 And the sea began to be stirred up because a strong wind was blowing.

19 When therefore they had rowed about three or four miles, they beheld Jesus walking on the sea and drawing near to the boat; and they were frightened.

20 But He said to them, "It is I; do not be afraid."

21 They were willing therefore to receive Him into the boat; and immediately the boat was at the land to which they were going.

22 The next day the multitude that stood on the other side of the sea saw that there was no other small boat there, except one, and that Jesus had not entered with His disciples into the boat, but that His disciples had gone away alone.

23 There came other small boats from Tiberias near to the place where they ate the bread after the Lord had given thanks.

24 When the multitude therefore saw that Jesus was not there, nor His disciples, they themselves got into the small boats, and came to Capernaum, seeking Jesus.

25 And when they found Him on the other side of the sea, they said to Him, "Rabbi, when did You get here?"

26 Jesus answered them and said, "Truly, truly, I say to you, you seek Me, not because you saw signs, but because you ate of the loaves, and were filled.

27 "Do not work for the food which perishes, but for the food which endures to eternal life, which the Son of Man shall give to you, for on Him the Father, even God, has set His seal."

28 They said therefore to Him, "What shall we do, that we may work the works of God?"

29 Jesus answered and said to them, "This is the work of God, that you believe in Him whom He has sent."

30 They said therefore to Him, "What then do You do for a sign, that we may see, and believe You? What work do You perform?

31 "Our fathers ate the manna in the wilderness; as it is written, 'HE GAVE THEM BREAD OUT OF HEAVEN TO EAT.'"

32 Jesus therefore said to them, "Truly, truly, I say to you, it is not Moses who has given you the bread out of heaven, but it is My Father who gives you the true bread out of heaven.

33"For the bread of God is that which comes down out of heaven, and gives life to the world."

34 They said therefore to Him, "Lord, evermore give us this bread."

35 Jesus said to them, "I am the bread of life; he who comes to Me shall not hunger, and he who believes in Me shall never thirst.

36 "But I said to you, that you have seen Me, and yet do not believe.

37 "All that the Father gives Me shall come to Me, and the one who comes to Me I will certainly not cast out.

38 "For I have come down from heaven, not to do My own will, but the will of Him who sent Me.

39 "And this is the will of Him who sent Me, that of all that He has given Me I lose nothing, but raise it up on the last day.

40 "For this is the will of My Father, that everyone who beholds the Son and believes in Him, may have eternal life; and I Myself will raise him up on the last day."

41 The Jews therefore were grumbling about Him, because He said, "I am the bread that came down out of heaven."

42 And they were saying, "Is not this Jesus, the son of Joseph, whose father and mother we know? How does He now say, 'I have come down out of heaven'?"

43 Jesus answered and said to them, "Do not grumble among yourselves.

44 "No one can come to Me, unless the Father who sent Me draws him; and I will raise him up on the last day.

45 "It is written in the prophets, 'AND THEY SHALL ALL BE TAUGHT OF GOD.' Everyone who has heard and learned from the Father, comes to Me.

46 "Not that any man has seen the Father, except the One who is from God; He has seen the Father.

47 "Truly, truly, I say to you, he who believes has eternal life.

48 "I am the bread of life.

49 "Your fathers ate the manna in the wilderness, and they died.

50 "This is the bread which comes down out of heaven, so that one may eat of it and not die.

51 "I am the living bread that came down out of heaven; if anyone eats of this bread, he shall live forever; and the bread also which I shall give for the life of the world is My flesh."

52 The Jews therefore began to argue with one another, saying, "How can this man give us His flesh to eat?"

53 Jesus therefore said to them, "Truly, truly, I say to you, unless you eat the flesh of the Son of Man and drink His blood, you have no life in yourselves.

54 "He who eats My flesh and drinks My blood has eternal life, and I will raise him up on the last day.

55 "For My flesh is true food, and My blood is true drink.

56 "He who eats My flesh and drinks My blood abides in Me, and I in him.

57 "As the living Father sent Me, and I live because of the Father, so he who eats Me, he also shall live because of Me.

58 "This is the bread which came down out of heaven; not as the fathers ate, and died, he who eats this bread shall live forever."

59 These things He said in the synagogue, as He taught in Capernaum.

60 Many therefore of His disciples, when they heard this said, "This is a difficult statement; who can listen to it?"

61 But Jesus, conscious that His disciples grumbled at this, said to them, "Does this cause you to stumble?

62 "What then if you should behold the Son of Man ascending where He was before?

63 "It is the Spirit who gives life; the flesh profits nothing; the words that I have spoken to you are spirit and are life.

64 "But there are some of you who do not believe." For Jesus knew from the beginning who they were who did not believe, and who it was that would betray Him.

65 And He was saying, "For this reason I have said to you, that no one can come to Me, unless it has been granted him from the Father."

66 As a result of this many of His disciples withdrew, and were not walking with Him anymore.

67 Jesus said therefore to the twelve, "You do not want to go away also, do you?"

68 Simon Peter answered Him, "Lord, to whom shall we go? You have words of eternal life.

69 "And we have believed and have come to know that You are the Holy One of God."

70 Jesus answered them, "Did I Myself not choose you, the twelve, and yet one of you is a devil?"

71 Now He meant Judas the son of Simon Iscariot, for he, one of the twelve, was going to betray Him.

Chapter 7

1 And after these things Jesus was walking in Galilee; for He was unwilling to walk in Judea, because the Jews were seeking to kill Him.

2 Now the feast of the Jews, the Feast of Booths, was at hand.

3 His brothers therefore said to Him, "Depart from here, and go into Judea, that Your disciples also may behold Your works which You are doing.

4 "For no one does anything in secret, when he himself seeks to be known publicly. If You do these things, show Yourself to the world."

5 For not even His brothers were believing in Him.

6 Jesus therefore said to them, "My time is not yet at hand, but your time is always opportune.

7 "The world cannot hate you; but it hates Me because I testify of it, that its deeds are evil.

8 "Go up to the feast yourselves; I do not go up to this feast because My time has not yet fully come."

9 And having said these things to them, He stayed in Galilee.

10 But when His brothers had gone up to the feast, then He Himself also went up, not publicly, but as it were, in secret.

11 The Jews therefore were seeking Him at the feast, and were saying, "Where is He?"

12 And there was much grumbling among the multitudes concerning Him; some were saying, "He is a good man"; others were saying, "No, on the contrary, He leads the multitude astray."

13 Yet no one was speaking openly of Him for fear of the Jews.

14 But when it was now the midst of the feast Jesus went up into the temple, and began to teach.

15 The Jews therefore were marveling, saying, "How has this man become learned, having never been educated?"

16 Jesus therefore answered them, and said, "My teaching is not Mine, but His who sent Me.

17 "If any man is willing to do His will, he shall know of the teaching, whether it is of God, or whether I speak from Myself.

18 "He who speaks from himself seeks his own glory; but He who is seeking the glory of the One who sent Him, He is true, and there is no unrighteousness in Him.

19 "Did not Moses give you the Law, and yet none of you carries out the Law? Why do you seek to kill Me?"

20 The multitude answered, "You have a demon! Who seeks to kill You?"

21 Jesus answered and said to them, "I did one deed, and you all marvel.

22 "On this account Moses has given you circumcision (not because it is from Moses, but from the fathers), and on the Sabbath you circumcise a man.

23 "If a man receives circumcision on the Sabbath that the Law of Moses may not be broken, are you angry with Me because I made an entire man well on the Sabbath?

24 "Do not judge according to appearance, but judge with righteous judgment."

25 Therefore some of the people of Jerusalem were saying, "Is this not the man whom they are seeking to kill?

26 "And look, He is speaking publicly, and they are saying nothing to Him. The rulers do not really know that this is the Christ, do they?

27 "However, we know where this man is from; but whenever the Christ may come, no one knows where He is from."

28 Jesus therefore cried out in the temple, teaching and saying, "You both know Me and know where I am from; and I have not come of Myself, but He who sent Me is true, whom you do not know.

29 "I know Him; because I am from Him, and He sent Me."

30 They were seeking therefore to seize Him; and no man laid his hand on Him, because His hour had not yet come.

31 But many of the multitude believed in Him; and they were saying, "When the Christ shall come, He will not perform more signs than those which this man has, will He?"

32 The Pharisees heard the multitude muttering these things about Him; and the chief priests and the Pharisees sent officers to seize Him.

33 Jesus therefore said, "For a little while longer I am with you, then I go to Him who sent Me.

34 "You shall seek Me, and shall not find Me; and where I am, you cannot come."

35 The Jews therefore said to one another, "Where does this man intend to go that we shall not find Him? He is not intending to go to the Dispersion among the Greeks, and teach the Greeks, is He?

36 "What is this statement that He said, 'You will seek Me, and will not find Me; and where I am, you cannot come'?"

37 Now on the last day, the great day of the feast, Jesus stood and cried out, saying, "If any man is thirsty, let him come to Me and drink.

38 "He who believes in Me, as the Scripture said, 'From his innermost being shall flow rivers of living water.'"

39 But this He spoke of the Spirit, whom those who believed in Him were to receive; for the Spirit was not yet given, because Jesus was not yet glorified.

40 Some of the multitude therefore, when they heard these words, were saying, "This certainly is the Prophet."

41 Others were saying, "This is the Christ." Still others were saying, "Surely the Christ is not going to come from Galilee, is He?

42 "Has not the Scripture said that the Christ comes from the off-spring of David, and from Bethlehem, the village where David was?"

43 So there arose a division in the multitude because of Him.

44 And some of them wanted to seize Him, but no one laid hands on Him.

45 The officers therefore came to the chief priests and Pharisees, and they said to them, "Why did you not bring Him?"

46 The officers answered, "Never did a man speak the way this man speaks."

47 The Pharisees therefore answered them, "You have not also been led astray, have you?

48 "No one of the rulers or Pharisees has believed in Him, has he?

49 "But this multitude which does not know the Law is accursed."

50 Nicodemus said to them (he who came to Him before, being one of them),

51 "Our Law does not judge a man, unless it first hears from him and knows what he is doing, does it?"

52 They answered and said to him, "You are not also from Galilee, are you? Search, and see that no prophet arises out of Galilee."

53 And everyone went to his home.

Chapter 8

1 But Jesus went to the Mount of Olives.

2 And early in the morning He came again into the temple, and all the people were coming to Him; and He sat down and began to teach them.

3 And the scribes and the Pharisees brought a woman caught in adultery, and having set her in the midst,

4 they said to Him, "Teacher, this woman has been caught in adultery, in the very act.

5 "Now in the Law Moses commanded us to stone such women; what then do You say?"

6 And they were saying this, testing Him, in order that they might have grounds for accusing Him. But Jesus stooped down, and with His finger wrote on the ground.

7 But when they persisted in asking Him, He straightened up, and said to them, "He who is without sin among you, let him be the first to throw a stone at her."

8 And again He stooped down, and wrote on the ground.

9 And when they heard it, they began to go out one by one, beginning with the older ones, and He was left alone, and the woman, where she was, in the midst.

10 And straightening up, Jesus said to her, "Woman, where are they? Did no one condemn you?"

11 And she said, "No one, Lord." And Jesus said, "Neither do I condemn you; go your way. From now on sin no more."]

12 Again therefore Jesus spoke to them, saying, "I am the light of the world; he who follows Me shall not walk in the darkness, but shall have the light of life."

13 The Pharisees therefore said to Him, "You are bearing witness of Yourself; Your witness is not true."

14 Jesus answered and said to them, "Even if I bear witness of Myself, My witness is true; for I know where I came from, and where I am going; but you do not know where I come from, or where I am going.

15 "You people judge according to the flesh; I am not judging anyone.

16 "But even if I do judge, My judgment is true; for I am not alone in it, but I and He who sent Me.

17 "Even in your law it has been written, that the testimony of two men is true.

18 "I am He who bears witness of Myself, and the Father who sent Me bears witness of Me."

19 And so they were saying to Him, "Where is Your Father?" Jesus answered, "You know neither Me, nor My Father; if you knew Me, you would know My Father also."

20 These words He spoke in the treasury, as He taught in the temple; and no one seized Him, because His hour had not yet come.

21 He said therefore again to them, "I go away, and you shall seek Me, and shall die in your sin; where I am going, you cannot come."

22 Therefore the Jews were saying, "Surely He will not kill Himself, will He, since He says, 'Where I am going, you cannot come'?"

23 And He was saying to them, "You are from below, I am from above; you are of this world, I am not of this world.

24 "I said therefore to you, that you shall die in your sins; for unless you believe that I am He, you shall die in your sins."

25 And so they were saying to Him, "Who are You?" Jesus said to them, "What have I been saying to you from the beginning?

26 "I have many things to speak and to judge concerning you, but He who sent Me is true; and the things which I heard from Him, these I speak to the world."

27 They did not realize that He had been speaking to them about the Father.

28 Jesus therefore said, "When you lift up the Son of Man, then you will know that I am He, and I do nothing on My own initiative, but I speak these things as the Father taught Me.

29 "And He who sent Me is with Me; He has not left Me alone, for I always do the things that are pleasing to Him."

30 As He spoke these things, many came to believe in Him.

31 Jesus therefore was saying to those Jews who had believed Him, "If you abide in My word, then you are truly disciples of Mine;

32 and you shall know the truth, and the truth shall make you free."

33 They answered Him, "We are Abraham's offspring, and have never yet been enslaved to anyone; how is it that You say, 'You shall become free'?"

34 Jesus answered them, "Truly, truly, I say to you, everyone who commits sin is the slave of sin.

35 "And the slave does not remain in the house forever; the son does remain forever.

36 "If therefore the Son shall make you free, you shall be free indeed.

37 "I know that you are Abraham's offspring; yet you seek to kill Me, because My word has no place in you.

38 "I speak the things which I have seen with My Father; therefore you also do the things which you heard from your father."

39 They answered and said to Him, "Abraham is our father." Jesus said to them, "If you are Abraham's children, do the deeds of Abraham.

40 "But as it is, you are seeking to kill Me, a man who has told you the truth, which I heard from God; this Abraham did not do.

41 "You are doing the deeds of your father." They said to Him, "We were not born of fornication; we have one Father, even God."

42 Jesus said to them, "If God were your Father, you would love Me; for I proceeded forth and have come from God, for I have not even come on My own initiative, but He sent Me.

43 "Why do you not understand what I am saying? It is because you cannot hear My word.

44 "You are of your father the devil, and you want to do the desires of your father. He was a murderer from the beginning, and does not stand in the truth, because there is no truth in him. Whenever he speaks a lie, he speaks from his own nature; for he is a liar, and the father of lies.

45 "But because I speak the truth, you do not believe Me.

46 "Which one of you convicts Me of sin? If I speak truth, why do you not believe Me?

47 "He who is of God hears the words of God; for this reason you do not hear them, because you are not of God."

48 The Jews answered and said to Him, "Do we not say rightly that You are a Samaritan and have a demon?"

49 Jesus answered, "I do not have a demon; but I honor My Father, and you dishonor Me.

50 "But I do not seek My glory; there is One who seeks and judges.

51 "Truly, truly, I say to you, if anyone keeps My word he shall never see death."

52 The Jews said to Him, "Now we know that You have a demon. Abraham died, and the prophets also; and You say, 'If anyone keeps My word, he shall never taste of death.'

53 "Surely You are not greater than our father Abraham, who died? The prophets died too; whom do You make Yourself out to be?"

54 Jesus answered, "If I glorify Myself, My glory is nothing; it is My Father who glorifies Me, of whom you say, 'He is our God';

55 and you have not come to know Him, but I know Him; and if I say that I do not know Him, I shall be a liar like you, but I do know Him, and keep His word.

56 "Your father Abraham rejoiced to see My day, and he saw it and was glad."

57 The Jews therefore said to Him, "You are not yet fifty years old, and have You seen Abraham?"

58 Jesus said to them, "Truly, truly, I say to you, before Abraham was born, I am."

59 Therefore they picked up stones to throw at Him; but Jesus hid Himself, and went out of the temple.

Chapter 9

1 And as He passed by, He saw a man blind from birth.

2 And His disciples asked Him, saying, "Rabbi, who sinned, this man or his parents, that he should be born blind?"

3 Jesus answered, "It was neither that this man sinned, nor his parents; but it was in order that the works of God might be displayed in him.

4 "We must work the works of Him who sent Me, as long as it is day; night is coming, when no man can work.

5 "While I am in the world, I am the light of the world."

6 When He had said this, He spat on the ground, and made clay of the spittle, and applied the clay to his eyes,

7 and said to him, "Go, wash in the pool of Siloam" (which is translated, Sent). And so he went away and washed, and came back seeing.

8 The neighbors therefore, and those who previously saw him as a beggar, were saying, "Is not this the one who used to sit and beg?"

9 Others were saying, "This is he," still others were saying, "No, but he is like him." He kept saying, "I am the one."

10 Therefore they were saying to him, "How then were your eyes opened?"

11 He answered, "The man who is called Jesus made clay, and anointed my eyes, and said to me, 'Go to Siloam, and wash'; so I went away and washed, and I received sight."

12 And they said to him, "Where is He?" He said, "I do not know."

13 They brought to the Pharisees him who was formerly blind.

14 Now it was a Sabbath on the day when Jesus made the clay, and opened his eyes.

15 Again, therefore, the Pharisees also were asking him how he received his sight. And he said to them, "He applied clay to my eyes, and I washed, and I see."

16 Therefore some of the Pharisees were saying, "This man is not from God, because He does not keep the Sabbath." But others were saying, "How can a man who is a sinner perform such signs?" And there was a division among them.

17 They said therefore to the blind man again, "What do you say about Him, since He opened your eyes?" And he said, "He is a prophet."

18 The Jews therefore did not believe it of him, that he had been blind, and had received sight, until they called the parents of the very one who had received his sight,

19 and questioned them, saying, "Is this your son, who you say was born blind? Then how does he now see?"

20 His parents answered them and said, "We know that this is our son, and that he was born blind;

21 but how he now sees, we do not know; or who opened his eyes, we do not know. Ask him; he is of age, he shall speak for himself."

22 His parents said this because they were afraid of the Jews; for the Jews had already agreed, that if anyone should confess Him to be Christ, he should be put out of the synagogue.

23 For this reason his parents said, "He is of age; ask him."

24 So a second time they called the man who had been blind, and said to him, "Give glory to God; we know that this man is a sinner."

25 He therefore answered, "Whether He is a sinner, I do not know; one thing I do know, that, whereas I was blind, now I see."

26 They said therefore to him, "What did He do to you? How did He open your eyes?"

27 He answered them, "I told you already, and you did not listen; why do you want to hear it again? You do not want to become His disciples too, do you?"

28 And they reviled him, and said, "You are His disciple, but we are disciples of Moses.

29 "We know that God has spoken to Moses; but as for this man, we do not know where He is from."

30 The man answered and said to them, "Well, here is an amazing thing, that you do not know where He is from, and yet He opened my eyes.

31 "We know that God does not hear sinners; but if anyone is God-fearing, and does His will, He hears him.

32 "Since the beginning of time it has never been heard that anyone opened the eyes of a person born blind.

33 "If this man were not from God, He could do nothing."

34 They answered and said to him, "You were born entirely in sins, and are you teaching us?" And they put him out.

35 Jesus heard that they had put him out; and finding him, He said, "Do you believe in the Son of Man?"

36 He answered and said, "And who is He, Lord, that I may believe in Him?"

37 Jesus said to him, "You have both seen Him, and He is the one who is talking with you."

38 And he said, "Lord, I believe." And he worshiped Him.

39 And Jesus said, "For judgment I came into this world, that those who do not see may see; and that those who see may become blind."

40 Those of the Pharisees who were with Him heard these things, and said to Him, "We are not blind too, are we?"

41 Jesus said to them, "If you were blind, you would have no sin; but since you say, 'We see,' your sin remains.

Chapter 10

1 "Truly, truly, I say to you, he who does not enter by the door into the fold of the sheep, but climbs up some other way, he is a thief and a robber.

2 "But he who enters by the door is a shepherd of the sheep.

3 "To him the doorkeeper opens, and the sheep hear his voice, and he calls his own sheep by name, and leads them out.

4 "When he puts forth all his own, he goes before them, and the sheep follow him because they know his voice.

5 "And a stranger they simply will not follow, but will flee from him, because they do not know the voice of strangers."

6 This figure of speech Jesus spoke to them, but they did not understand what those things were which He had been saying to them.

7 Jesus therefore said to them again, "Truly, truly, I say to you, I am the door of the sheep.

8 "All who came before Me are thieves and robbers, but the sheep did not hear them.

9 "I am the door; if anyone enters through Me, he shall be saved, and shall go in and out, and find pasture.

10 "The thief comes only to steal, and kill, and destroy; I came that they might have life, and might have it abundantly.

11 "I am the good shepherd; the good shepherd lays down His life for the sheep.

12 "He who is a hireling, and not a shepherd, who is not the owner of the sheep, beholds the wolf coming, and leaves the sheep, and flees, and the wolf snatches them, and scatters them.

13 "He flees because he is a hireling, and is not concerned about the sheep.

14 "I am the good shepherd; and I know My own, and My own know Me,

15 even as the Father knows Me and I know the Father; and I lay down My life for the sheep.

16 "And I have other sheep, which are not of this fold; I must bring them also, and they shall hear My voice; and they shall become one flock with one shepherd.

17 "For this reason the Father loves Me, because I lay down My life that I may take it again.

18 "No one has taken it away from Me, but I lay it down on My own initiative. I have authority to lay it down, and I have authority to take it up again. This commandment I received from My Father."

19 There arose a division again among the Jews because of these words.

20 And many of them were saying, "He has a demon and is insane. Why do you listen to Him?"

21 Others were saying, "These are not the sayings of one demon-possessed. A demon cannot open the eyes of the blind, can he?"

22 At that time the Feast of the Dedication took place at Jerusalem;

23 it was winter, and Jesus was walking in the temple in the portico of Solomon.

24 The Jews therefore gathered around Him, and were saying to Him, "How long will You keep us in suspense? If You are the Christ, tell us plainly."

25 Jesus answered them, "I told you, and you do not believe; the works that I do in My Father's name, these bear witness of Me.

26 "But you do not believe, because you are not of My sheep.

27 "My sheep hear My voice, and I know them, and they follow Me;

28 and I give eternal life to them, and they shall never perish; and no one shall snatch them out of My hand.

29 "My Father, who has given them to Me, is greater than all; and no one is able to snatch them out of the Father's hand.

30 "I and the Father are one."

31 The Jews took up stones again to stone Him.

32 Jesus answered them, "I showed you many good works from the Father; for which of them are you stoning Me?"

33 The Jews answered Him, "For a good work we do not stone You, but for blasphemy; and because You, being a man, make Yourself out to be God."

34 Jesus answered them, "Has it not been written in your Law, 'I SAID, YOU ARE GODS'?

35 "If he called them gods, to whom the word of God came (and the Scripture cannot be broken),

36 do you say of Him, whom the Father sanctified and sent into the world, 'You are blaspheming,' because I said, 'I am the Son of God'?

37 "If I do not do the works of My Father, do not believe Me;

38 but if I do them, though you do not believe Me, believe the works, that you may know and understand that the Father is in Me, and I in the Father."

39 Therefore they were seeking again to seize Him, and He eluded their grasp.

40 And He went away again beyond the Jordan to the place where John was first baptizing, and He was staying there.

41 And many came to Him and were saying, "While John performed no sign, yet everything John said about this man was true."

42 And many believed in Him there.

I Did It!

I discovered more about the Bible for myself!

My name _____

My address _____

STREET OR P.O. BOX

_____
CITY   STATE   ZIP CODE

The study I did was _____
(TITLE OF BOOK)

My favorite thing about it was _____.

Here's the grown-up who knows I did it:

_____
(MOM'S OR DAD'S SIGNATURE)

*Mail this postcard. We have something
special we want to send you!*

YES, I WANT TO GROW SPIRITUALLY.
TELL ME MORE ABOUT

PRECEPT MINISTRIES INTERNATIONAL

Name _____

Address _____

City _____

State _____ Postal Code _____

Country _____

Daytime phone ( ) _____

Email address _____

Fax ( ) _____

Evening phone ( ) _____

PLEASE SEND ME INFO ON:

❏ Learning how to study the Bible
❏ Bible study material
❏ Radio Programs
❏ TV Programs
❏ Israel Bible Study Tour
❏ Paul's Epistles Study Tour to Greece
❏ Men's Conferences
❏ Women's Conferences
❏ Teen Conferences
❏ Couples' Conferences
❏ Other _____
❏ I want to partner with Precept Ministries
ENCLOSED IS MY DONATION FOR $ _____

P.O. Box 182218 • Chattanooga, TN 37422-7218
(800) 763-8280 • (423) 892-6814 • Radio/TV (800) 763-1990
Fax: (423) 894-2449 • www.precept.org • Email: info@precept.org

BUSINESS REPLY MAIL
FIRST-CLASS MAIL   PERMIT NO. 48   CHATTANOOGA TN

POSTAGE WILL BE PAID BY ADDRESSEE

PRECEPT MINISTRIES
P O BOX 182218
CHATTANOOGA TN 37422-9901

NO POSTAGE
NECESSARY
IF MAILED
IN THE
UNITED STATES

BUSINESS REPLY MAIL
FIRST-CLASS MAIL   PERMIT NO. 48   CHATTANOOGA TN

POSTAGE WILL BE PAID BY ADDRESSEE

PRECEPT MINISTRIES
P O BOX 182218
CHATTANOOGA TN 37422-9901